"*Care*, by Dr. Dwayne Bond, is a gift to the body of Christ! With wisdom as warm as it is wise, Dr. Bond takes us on a journey deep into the heart of what it truly means to care for one another as the family of God. He's crafted a masterful guide, both practical and profound, to build a church culture where loving relationships fuel spiritual formation and where hearts mature in Christ-like love. Read it, teach it, share it. Use it in small groups, and let this book bless everyone in your congregation."

DR. DOUG LOGAN, JR., President of Grimké Seminary and College; Author, *On the Block*; Coauthor, *The Soul-Winning Church* and *The Least, the Last and the Lost*

"Churches are meant to be visible communities of love, support, encouragement, and care—because we know the Savior who 'cares for you' (1 Peter 5:7). Dwayne Bond is one of the most caring men you could ever meet. He lives the biblical principles and practical examples that fill his excellent and needed book *Care*. Take this Christ-centered, edifying, and authentic book to heart because someone will need you soon."

J.A. MEDDERS, General Editor, NewChurches.com; Author, *The Risen King: 40 Devotions for Easter with C.H. Spurgeon*; *Humble Calvinism*; Coauthor, *The Soul-Winning Church*

"The local church is God's chosen place for care. Our ability to care for others is rooted in and fueled by our understanding of the love Christ has for us. In this book, Dwayne Bond explains how to experience unity through genuine love and by caring like Jesus. Throughout the pages you will find yourself saying, 'Yes and Amen!' I highly recommend that your entire church read this book, as together you seek to cultivate authentic community and foster a culture of grace."

SHAUNA VAN DYKE, Executive Director, The Association of Biblical Counselors (ABC); Care and Leadership Development Minister, The Mount Church, Keller, TX

T0343669

"This book is a must-read for church leaders and small groups! Dwayne Bond brilliantly unpacks why loving the church truly matters and how we can overcome the barriers that often keep us from caring for one another. Each chapter gives hopeful direction on how the church, with all its diversity, can become a loving family. This is a book rich with practical insights that will deepen our love for Christ and one another in powerful ways."

ELIZA HUIE, Director of Counseling, McLean Bible Church; Author, *Trauma Aware: A Christian's Guide to Help and Care* and *I'm Stressed: A Path from Pressure to Peace*

"Dr. Dwayne Bond has provided an accessible and insightful guide on how to care for the people in our churches. More than just principles, here you will find practical guidance for how to minister the love of Christ to his people—no matter your context."

KYLE WORLEY, Author, *Home with God: Our Union with Christ*

"Dr. Bond is a master at combining care and counseling within the church community in his latest work, *Care: Loving Your Church by Walking Through Life Together*. This literary gem encourages and equips churches on how to love each other as God has instructed while living on mission together. The Scripture, reflections at the end of chapters and social and counseling references make this book all-encompassing as it relates to creating a counseling culture within the church."

JEROME GAY JR., Pastor; Author, *Church Hurt: Holding the Church Accountable and Helping Hurt People Heal*

"Pastor Dwayne Bond has crafted a beautiful blend of rich theological truth and practical church-based living. That blending in no way surprises me because for three decades I've watched Pastor Bond live out truth-in-love in the context of Christian community. I highly recommend *Care* for all those who care about living life together in the church."

BOB KELLEMEN, Author, 25 books including *Gospel-Centered Counseling: How Christ Changes Lives*

"One of the blessings of being a child of the living God is that we are not saved to be alone but saved to be part of a people who have all received the gracious, merciful, loving care of our Father in Christ Jesus. And one of the joys is that we get to be part of showing and experiencing that care through and to each other. In this wonderful addition to the 'Love Your Church' series, Dwayne encourages us to see what it looks like to truly be a church that cares, loves, and carries each other's burdens like Jesus in a culture that is divided, fractured, and in desperate need of gospel hope. Stimulating, challenging, and wonderfully encouraging!"

STEVE ROBINSON, Senior Pastor, Cornerstone Church, Liverpool, UK; Dean, Grimké Europe; Author, *Serve: Loving Your Church with Your Heart, Time and Gifts*

"Dr. Bond has created a work of profound and practical significance by teaching us how the church has been divinely designed to care for one another. I am grateful to have a resource written for the church that so thoroughly addresses the ongoing needs that only the church can provide!"

RONNIE MARTIN, Director, Leader Care and Renewal for Harbor Network; Pastor-in-Residence, Redeemer Community Church, Bloomington, IN; Coauthor, *The Unhurried Pastor*

"Dwayne expertly weaves together practical strategies with profound biblical truths, encouraging us to be vessels of hope and healing in a world that desperately needs it. His emphasis on hospitality, service, and love resonates deeply, reminding us that our faith is most vividly expressed through our actions. This book is a clarion call for believers to rise up and demonstrate the love of Christ in tangible ways, making him visible to those around us. I wholeheartedly recommend it to anyone seeking to deepen their understanding of Christian community and the vital role we play in reflecting God's love."

RACHAEL ROSSER-SCHULTE, Director, Restore Christian Counseling

care

DWAYNE BOND

Care:
Loving Your Church by Walking through Life Together
© Dwayne Bond, 2025

Published by:
The Good Book Company

thegoodbook.com | thegoodbook.co.uk
thegoodbook.com.au | thegoodbook.co.nz | thegoodbook.co.in

Unless otherwise indicated, Scripture quotations are from The Holy Bible,
English Standard Version (ESV), copyright © 2001 by Crossway, a publishing
ministry of Good News Publishers. Used by permission. All rights reserved.

All rights reserved. Except as may be permitted by the Copyright Act, no part
of this publication may be reproduced in any form or by any means without
prior permission from the publisher.

Dwayne Bond has asserted his right under the Copyright, Designs and Patents
Act 1988 to be identified as author of this work.

Original series cover design by Faceout Studio | Art direction and design by
André Parker

ISBN: 9781784988722 | JOB-008116 |Printed in India

CONTENTS

FOREWORD

BY JONATHAN D. HOLMES

The longer I am in counseling ministry, the more and more committed I find myself to realizing the beauty of and opportunities for care in the local church. Every week I hear stories of individuals, couples, and families struggling to think through the hardships and brokenness of life. Stories of grief and loss, of betrayal and heartache: stories where the unending pressures and troubles of life seem to press in as we seek to press on.

It's at times like these that I find myself needing to be reminded of simple truths from God's word. We all need a good reminder from time to time, don't we? The apostle Peter says as much in 2 Peter 1:13: he wants to "stir [us] up by way of reminder." It's an apt point. Sometimes we can get complacent about the reality that God saved us and placed us in the body of Christ. At other times we can get cynical about the body of Christ, focusing more on how our church has let us down or hurt us than the beauty of broken individuals coming together to declare the glory of the Lord.

My friend Dwayne follows in the footsteps of Peter and many others as he seeks to remind us of familiar truths but ones that we are quick to forget in the busyness and bustle of life. With a pastor's heart and a counselor's touch, Dwayne calls the church to its most organic mission—living out the one-anothers of the New Testament. How we live and care for one another in the body of Christ is one of the most distinctive ways in which believers testify to the gospel.

Jesus says in John 13:35, "By this all people will know that you are my disciples, if you have love for one another." The New Testament ethic of love is like a diamond. It shines and is beautiful in all its many facets, from service and prayer to greeting and bearing with one another's burdens.

Dwayne has given us a gift in this brief but potent work. He calls everyday people to be on the frontlines of caring for one another and, in turn, caring for the local communities they find themselves in. I, for one, am eager to see this ordinary vision of caring and compassionate living transform local churches across the country and across the globe. Isn't that what we all long and hope for, after all?

Jonathan D. Holmes
Founder and Executive Director,
Fieldstone Counseling

INTRODUCTION

Imagine a church that really, truly cares for one another. What would that look like?

A church where every person—with all their flaws, idiosyncrasies, and fragilities—is not just tolerated but embraced.

A church where no one feels invisible or excluded, but each person is a cherished part of the whole.

Picture a church saturated with empathy, where members share the burdens of one another, and the joys of each become the joys of all.

Imagine a church where love is not just talked about but is a tangible reality, weaving its way through every interaction, every gesture, and every prayer so that each individual feels valued and included.

A church where Christ's teaching resounds, and Christ's kindness reigns, and all are welcomed into the warm embrace of community without prejudice.

That would be a truly caring church.

That's the kind of church we all want to belong to.

But if we're honest, we know that our churches often fall short of that ideal. When we look at our own hearts, we know that *we* often fall short.

Don't get me wrong: your church likely does many things well. Yet I know from my own experience that too often, the harsh realities of human frailty and sin cast shadows upon the light of love. Hearts once eager for fellowship grow cold in the face of unmet expectations and longings. It's easy for people to fall through the cracks, despite our best efforts; or for us to become so busy with rosters and programs that we lose sight of the needs around us. Or maybe you find yourself drifting along at the edge of church life, feeling lonely and disillusioned.

In the frenzy of local-church life, it is easy to overlook the simple yet profound command that Jesus gave to his disciples in John 13:34: "A new commandment I give to you, that you love one another: just as I have loved you, you also are to love one another." The way we care for one another in the local church should be of utmost importance to us because it's of utmost importance to Jesus.

So, how do we become more like the caring church I just described? What does it look like to love one another as Jesus commands? Where will we find the focus and power to live up to his calling? That's what this book will address.

As we embark on this journey together, we'll be reminded of the radical nature of Christ's love and the transformative power it holds for our relationships with other believers. I will challenge us to move beyond mere surface-level interactions and instead cultivate an authentic culture of understanding, kindness, and generosity within our church community. That's what I've been trying to do for the last 30+ years as a church planter and pastor. And that's what I hope to help you do, through practical examples and biblical principles.

As we delve deeper into the pages of this book, we'll be challenged to emulate the example set by Jesus himself, who demonstrated the ultimate act of love through his sacrificial death on the cross. Just as he laid down his life for us, so too are we called to lay down our lives for one another, showing kindness, patience, and forgiveness to all in need. Not only are we called; we are equipped. By his Spirit, Jesus empowers us to love one another.

May this book catalyze deeper relationships, stronger communities, and a more vibrant expression of God's love within our midst. Together, let us strive to fulfill the command of Jesus to love one another as he has loved us.

1. WHY LOVING THE CHURCH MATTERS

The first Christian who taught me to how to care for others was my grandmother.

From the ages of nine to sixteen, I spent summers in the small city of Roanoke, Virginia, with my grandparents. It felt like a world away from the suburbs of Maryland, just outside of Washington, D.C., where I lived for the rest of the year.

My friends couldn't understand why I'd disappear to the country to be with old people.

The thing is, as a latch-key kid, outside of playing kickball, tackle football, and hide-and-go-seek, there wasn't much to do at home during the summer. So, instead, I spent the summer months enjoying my grandparents' company, eating delicious meals and hearing countless stories about family history. I could be with both of my grandparents and have their undivided time, attention, and love—particularly from my grandmother.

My parents' home was fun-loving yet tempestuous—tensions over money, communication, and other disagreements were a frequent part of the relational flow of the home. Both of my parents worked for the federal government. My mother worked the normal nine-to-five for 30 years. My father worked the night shift and drove a taxicab during the day and on the weekends for extra money. Neither of them were Christian, but they instilled within me a sense of morality and a strong work ethic.

Yet my grandmother's home was so different. She loved Jesus—and that love exuded from her towards others. Care and compassion flowed from her. You knew you were loved by her. People from church and the community would unexpectedly stop by the house at any time, and I'd see her pour forth hospitality towards them. She was thoughtful, kind, considerate, and patient. She served the elderly, sick, blind, poor, disabled, and mentally ill. She was devoted to her church family. She was like my very own Mother Theresa. I didn't understand why she would do what she did for people. At the time, I assumed that all grandmothers must be like this. But what I grew to learn was that she was actively living out her faith in, and love for, Jesus Christ.

My grandmother gave me my first view of Christ. Years later, when I got on my knees on my dorm room floor at the University of Maryland after a close friend shared the gospel with me, it finally clicked. My grandmother's life suddenly made sense. Everything that I saw her do flashed across the eyes of my heart. I needed the Jesus that she knew and loved.

MAKING CHRIST VISIBLE

This book is about how church communities can better care for and love one another. Why does this matter? It matters because, as my grandmother's example showed, the life and love of Christ are made visible by those who love like him.

On the night before he died, Jesus told his disciples:

> A new commandment I give to you, that you love one another: just as I have loved you, you also are to love one another. By this all people will know that you are my disciples, if you have love for one another.
>
> (John 13:34-35)

Jesus says, Love as I have loved you. Give your life, energy, time, and attention away for the good of other people, as I've given to you.

That last part is crucial. It's interesting that when Jesus said these words, he had just finished washing the disciples' feet, graciously loving and serving each one of them—including Judas, who was about to betray him. What he asked of his disciples was something that he himself modeled and demonstrated—all through his life, but supremely in his death.

To love like Jesus starts with being keenly aware of how he has loved us.

And how did he love us? He sacrificed himself for those who didn't deserve his sacrifice. He didn't set his love on those who deserved it but on those who didn't—including you and including me. Rather than shrinking from our sin-stained state, he came close, taking the form of a servant to walk among us, and stopping at nothing—not even the cross—to make us clean.

So, as recipients of the love of God, we are to love one another. 1 John 4:7-11 says:

> *Beloved, let us love one another, for love is from God, and whoever loves has been born of God and knows God. Anyone who does not love does not know God, because God is love. In this the love of God was made manifest among us, that God sent his only Son into the world, so that we might live through him. In this is love, not that we have loved God but that he loved us and sent his Son to be the propitiation for our sins. Beloved, if God so loved us, we also ought to love one another.*

John goes on:

> *If anyone says, "I love God," and hates his brother, he is a liar; for he who does not love his brother whom he has seen cannot love God whom he has not seen. (v 20)*

A profession of love for God can't coexist with hatred of someone whom God loves. Christians should be the most loving people on the planet. We love because he first loved us (v 19). Experiencing the love and grace of God compels us to love our brothers and sisters within the church family, and our neighbors outside of it (Matthew 22:39).

I find this so challenging: as a believer, I can't say that I love God and not love his people. This requires that we assess our relationships honestly and what they reflect about how we really think about God. This isn't just about warm, fuzzy feelings: the word encourages us to love not in word or talk but in deed and in truth (1 John 3:18). If I profess to know Jesus and have been saved by him, then it will show up tangibly in how I treat those around me.

It's a church loving like Jesus that will get the world noticing Jesus. My grandmother's life was one of obedience to Jesus' command in John 13:35. As I grew up, because of her love, I did indeed come to understand that she was Jesus' disciple, just as he had promised.

When God's people love one another, the world witnesses God at work. Loving one another matters because it showcases who we really are.

HOW LOVE LOOKS

So far, so good. But talking about love can sometimes start to feel pretty abstract. What does love look like exactly? When the world looks at the church, what kind of love should they see?

That's what we'll explore in the chapters that follow. But to start us off, consider Romans 12:9-10:

Let love be genuine. Abhor what is evil; hold fast to what is good. Love one another with brotherly affection. Outdo one another in showing honor.

This passage tells us several things about what love looks like.

First, it tells us that our love for one another should be "genuine" (v 9). That is, not situational, conditional, seasonal, or partial but sincere and honest. If you love someone, you demonstrate it in how you treat them. Too often we can be all smiles and flattery to someone's face, and moments later be grumbling about them in our hearts or gossiping about them behind their backs. A love that isn't genuine isn't really love.

Second, Paul says that genuine love hates evil and holds to good. When we love someone, we want what's best for them—and it's God who shows us what that is. We're to look to his word to tell us what is for our good (and cling to it) and what will ultimately destroy us (and run from it). And we're to help our brothers and sisters to do the same. What is good for someone won't always be the same as that which seems to make them happy in the moment, or which keeps a superficial peace. Relationships of real love involve heartfelt encouragements and hard conversations.

Third, when the world looks at us, they should see that we are devoted to one another. As fellow members in the church, we are encouraged to "love one another with brotherly affection" (v 10). Jesus wants us to love one another as brothers and sisters: to stick by one another as we would our biological family.

Fourth, our aim should be to "outdo one another in showing honor". God calls Christians to lead the way in honoring one another with eagerness. An honor culture should burst forth from the church.

The word "honor" means respect, esteem, and reverence. We aren't called only to love one another but also to demonstrate the highest amount of respect possible for one another. The Scripture says, "Do nothing from selfish ambition or conceit, but in humility count others more significant than yourselves" (Philippians 2:3). Put other peoples' interests above your own. Love one another in the way that Jesus loved us.

Genuine love—love that is devoted, committed, respectful, and true to God's word—is to be the hallmark of our relationships within the church. And when Christians love one another like that, strangers who come into our midst can't help but notice. Our churches increasingly become places where everyone can receive love and care in the name of the Lord Jesus.

THE WITNESS TO CULTURE

Several years ago, my church moved into a new building. As soon as we could, we planned an event that would allow us to introduce ourselves to the surrounding community.

We were eager to demonstrate to our neighbors that we are God's church, planted in the community to serve them. As the date approached, church members got excited about it, and a host of people made themselves available to serve.

The event was called Community Day. We invited neighbors and businesses in the community, friends, co-workers, and family to enjoy a time of free food, games, music, and conversation.

To help spread the word about the event, a small group from our church gathered on two Saturdays prior to the event to walk around the neighborhood, passing out flyers to people and business owners. Our hope was that we would have hundreds of people attend. Burgers, hotdogs, and sodas were purchased. Games were selected. Volunteers were assigned tasks. We were pumped!

Finally, Community Day arrived. Although, in the end, we didn't see hundreds from the community attend, there were a few visitors who unexpectedly showed up and gifted us with their unique presence.

In particular, two women pulled into the parking lot and got out of their car. As they opened the door, it was quickly apparent that something was different about them. As I glanced at them, I noticed that the car was packed with clutter. I thought that this was odd, but I didn't know what to think. I warmly greeted them and told them that we were glad to have them. In a matter of minutes, they made themselves a plate and were enjoying some of the burgers and hotdogs that we were cooking on the grill. As our people began getting to know them, it sadly became evident that they were homeless and living out of their car. It all began to make sense.

It didn't matter that these women were wearing tattered clothes, living out of their car, and clearly in need; our church members sought to draw them into their conversations and make them feel welcome. God's people were showing Christ's love to them, serving them, and offering them sincere kindness. It reminded me of the love and hospitality of my godly grandmother. I thought to myself, *Wow, this is our church!* I was so encouraged to know that these women felt at home! What a blessing. We didn't need hundreds to be present. We had the opportunity to demonstrate love and care for the people God had brought to us.

As the day continued, I saw Ms. Diana, a godly 65-year-old woman, talking to another guest who sat sheepishly in a chair beside her. It was clear that her confidence in herself was very low. But Ms. Diana was patiently talking to her like she was her best friend. Ms. Diana is a sweet, kind, and tender-hearted woman who would give the shirt off her back for anyone. As she sat next to this woman, I honestly wondered what they were talking about.

Quickly, the word spread among our church community that Ms. Diana was sharing the gospel with this woman, who was unfortunately homeless as well. The woman was listening to Ms. Diana's every word. After a few minutes, I noticed that she was happily eating a burger and a hotdog while intently listening. More than 25 minutes passed... As they continued talking, I was praying and asking God to please save her soul and use Ms. Diana's words and witness to bring her into the kingdom. Privately, our people began to pray for this woman's soul. *God, please save her! Please, Lord!* As people served her more food and made sure that she had all that she desired to eat, I saw Christian hospitality at work. What a joy to behold!

Well, God saved her! Hallelujah! Shortly afterward, I was asked to come to meet her. When I approached her, I told her that I was so glad that she was here, and she smiled and said, "Thank you for having me." Caring for this homeless woman as the event ended became the immediate priority of our church community. Where was she going to go from here? How could we make sure that she had what she needed and even a place to stay? Calls were made to find her housing resources. People prepared her a bag of food. Love was being poured out on our tattered yet beautiful neighbor!

Before I left to go home, I told her that she was more than welcome to come to our worship service the next day. She said, "I'll be there."

Honestly, I didn't know if she would come. I've engaged with homeless people before and was skeptical. But on Sunday, as I was greeting guests at the door after the service, she came up to me smiling and said, "Thank you for having me; I enjoyed myself, and I'm coming next week." My heart was so full. I felt tears welling up in my eyes... The love of God had moved through his people and was on display. By God's grace, a soul was saved. The church family loved this woman who didn't fit in, who wasn't middle-class or dressed like everyone else. She started out as our unexpected guest but is now our sister in Christ. The unconditional love from Ms. Diana and our church family created a pathway for this woman to meet Jesus.

Please don't think for one minute that our church is perfect. Or that things like that happen for us every week! But when a church loves and cares for one another, and then invites outsiders in, the world can experience something of Jesus' love through his people.

ACTION STEPS

- Reflect on Romans 12:9-10. Which of these commands do you most want to grow in as you continue to read this book?

- Identify one church member who is an example to you in caring for God's people, in a way that my grandmother or Ms. Diana was to me. Reach out to tell them how much they encourage you.

- Before you leave for church this Sunday, ask the Spirit to give you eyes to see who might especially need your kindness and care.

2. WHAT GETS IN THE WAY OF CARING FOR ONE ANOTHER?

Aside from my grandmother, the Christian who had the biggest impact on my journey to faith was a student in my fraternity at the University of Maryland. His name was Alan. He became one of my closest friends. We ate together. We shopped at the grocery store together. We cooked meals together. We left fraternity parties together. We were inseparable. He was different from anyone I had encountered in the fraternity. He was genuine, kindhearted, caring, loving, and pleasant. He didn't curse, get drunk, smoke marijuana, or chase women. He was a different dude. He was my guy! We quickly formed a trusting friendship. I knew that he cared for me, and he knew that I cared for him.

One evening after class, back in our eleven-by-eleven foot dorm room, my life changed forever. After talking about how we would prepare a pot of homemade spaghetti, Alan shared the gospel with me. I can't remember what the link to the spaghetti was—but his explanation of the gospel was simple, clear, and to the point. He said, "You and I are sinners and in need of a Savior. Jesus loves you and died on the cross for your sins." He then asked me if I wanted to receive Jesus as my Lord and Savior. Broken, convicted, and overwhelmed by God's love, I dropped to my knees and placed my faith in Christ. Then I stood up, brushed my knees, and felt free.

But that was only the start. Shortly after my conversion, my friend introduced me to other Christians and invited me to a Bible study held at a local church. Every Wednesday night, we gathered with other Christian college-aged students and grew together in the Scriptures. I quickly felt at home. The love of Christ was radiant from my new tribe. They were interested in each other's lives; they asked good questions; they helped each other out practically; they rallied around when someone was struggling; they prayed for one another. It was beautiful.

My friend also invited me to his church on a Sunday and introduced me to what would become my new spiritual family. It had the same atmosphere of love and care as the Bible study, but multiplied across generations, as people looked out for and looked after one another through life's many different joys and challenges: from new babies to aging bodies and everything in between. It didn't take long for me to want to be part of it. Just like the Bible study, it felt like family to me. A year later, I served in the Student Ministry, helping other teenagers and college students experience the truth of God and showing them how to apply the Scriptures to everyday life.

Since then, I've had the joy of being part of a number of devoted, caring church families. But even now, as I look back on those early years of my Christian life, I can't help but smile. It was all so new and different from anything I'd ever experienced.

But sometimes I wonder: What if it hadn't been? What would have happened if each of these people had been more devoted to what mattered to them than what mattered to God? What if my fraternity brother had been more devoted to chasing popularity and women on campus rather than loving Jesus and people like myself? What if those Christian students had been more interested in proving themselves right than putting themselves out for one another? What if those church members had been more concerned with the comfort and preferences of their own nuclear families instead of the church family? Would that 18-year-old new Christian have become the pastor I am today?

IDOL LOVE

In the last chapter, we looked at Jesus' command to his followers to love one another. Yet I'm sure we can all think of times when we have failed to do that. Why is that?

Put simply, it's because we're loving other things instead. These are what the New Testament calls idols. Idols are good things we love more than God. But there's a second knock-on effect too: gravitating to our idols of choice hinders us from loving one another. Without knowing it, we become seduced into loving our idols more than we love people. When we pursue idols that we think will rescue us from something we fear or provide us with something we want, that creates a barrier to loving one another.

That's one of the reasons why the New Testament is full of warnings against idolatry. In 1 Corinthians 10:7, Paul says, "Do not be idolaters as some of them were; as it is written, 'The people sat down to eat and drink and rose up to play.'" Here, Paul quotes from Exodus 32:6—a chapter describing one of the most shameful times in Israel's Old Testament history. God was giving Moses the law on Mount Sinai. While Moses was away, the people of Israel became restless. Desiring to exchange God for something tangible that they could control, they summoned Aaron to make them gods who would go before them. Aaron collected up their gold possessions and made a golden calf for them to worship and make sacrifices to. Back up on the mountain, knowing what they were doing, the Lord told Moses to go down the mountain to the people of Israel. Moses returned angry. He burned the golden calf, ground it to powder, scattered it on the water, and made the people of Israel drink it (v 20).

Why is Paul referencing the story of Exodus 32 in his letter to the Corinthians? Paul is telling the Corinthian church not to follow the example of their forefathers who worshiped idols. He is warning them not to worship any non-god thing as if it is God or make sacrifices to it. Why? Paul knows that the enemy desires to rule our hearts. He wants to capture our allegiance. He wants us to disregard the worship of God in exchange of the false worship of a pseudo-savior.

That is still true for believers today. We may not be tempted to make statues to bow down to, but we frequently worship other things.

For instance, many of us seek to be perceived as significant. Social media thrives on people seeking to be noticed or deemed significant. There's nothing inherently wrong with social media. However, if our intention as we interact with others—be that online or offline—is to be accepted, approved of, and regarded as significant, we could be slipping into idolatry. We are called to worship God and not the affirmation of others. If we conduct relationships solely with a view to how good they make us feel, we won't love others—we'll simply use them.

Comfort and security are other idols that we become susceptible to. We give our full attention to ensuring that we gain and maintain a position of comfort and security. This pursuit can, even without us knowing, capture our devotion and create a pathway to idolatry for us. The Scripture teaches us that our comfort and security are in Christ and not in the things of this world. If we idolize comfort and security, we won't be willing to take risks or make sacrifices in the name of love.

The desire for power can lead us into idolatry as well. This is when we want to have control and power at all costs.

We pursue it, long for it, dream of it, and make sacrifices to have it. However, when we surrender to God's power, we recognize that we don't have to be powerful and are freed to humbly serve others, rather than seeking to control them.

Lastly, we worship money. This too is idolatry. The love of money is a root of all kinds of evil (1 Timothy 6:10). Scripture calls us to trust in God's provision with contentment (Hebrews 13:5). Money is to be used as a means of acquiring what we need—but it isn't intended to be worshiped. If our minds are busily preoccupied with earning money and spending money, we'll be blind to the needs of others right in front of us—and much less inclined to meet those needs with generosity.

It's no wonder, then, that in 1 Corinthians 10:14, Paul says, "Therefore, my beloved, flee from idolatry." He says, *Move quickly from one point to another to avoid the imminent danger of idolatry.* He doesn't say, *Reason with idols.* He doesn't say, *Manage idols.* He says, "Flee."

Why does Paul implore Christians to flee from idolatry? Because idolatry ruins our Christian witness and hinders us from loving Jesus and others. This is deadly serious. Paul is seeking to align Christians with the words and life of Jesus, calling us to love Jesus and others more than our idol of choice.

The Bible sets a high bar for how we are to love one another within the church (Hebrews 13:1). We are to love one another with brotherly affection (Romans 12:10). We're to love one another unconditionally and genuinely, as brothers and sisters who all belong to the family of God. We're to be zealous, fervent, and selfless in our love for one another. We're to care for one another practically and provide for each other's needs. We can't bring our idols along with us; there just isn't room.

How are we really doing at loving one another? How many newly converted college students—or single moms or struggling older saints or discouraged disciples— could have their trajectory transformed by a brother or sister who is ready to love them, and love Jesus, more than they love their comfort, security, prestige, power, money, race, personal opinions, control, and material things? When we turn from these things and toward others, beautiful things can happen.

We can't love God and idols. We can't love one another and idols. Might it be that our love for one another—and our witness to the culture—is being stifled by the non-god things that we love more? Sadly, I think so.

We're not done yet. Let's dig a little deeper into how our idolatry plays out in three areas that are particularly pertinent in our cultural moment.

Racism

During the Civil Rights Movement of the 20th century, advocate Martin Luther King Jr. described 11 a.m. on a

Sunday as "the most segregated hour in America."[1] Sixty years later, this is still very much the case. A recent study found that 86% of American churches have no significant racial diversity.[2] If, as some people believe, racism doesn't exist, then why aren't our churches more diverse?

In a racially divided culture, we have a wonderful opportunity to put the beautiful diversity of the gospel on display in church. Black people can demonstrate love for White people in church. Asian people can demonstrate love for Black people. White people can do life with and experience the richness of other cultures in church.

Think about it: is there part of you that doesn't want to worship with someone who doesn't look like you? What's going on inside your heart even as I ask this question? Could it be that you are prizing the idol of your own comfort or privilege or sense of "rightness" at the expense of brothers and sisters in Christ? Are people who don't look like you not worthy of your love?

Hopefully, you know the answer to that last question is "Yes, they are!" But very often, we find ourselves naturally gravitating towards people like us and away from those who look or speak or act or dress differently. All of us need to fight against this instinct. The next time that someone who doesn't look like you visits your

---

1 "The Most Segregated Hour in America - Martin Luther King Jr", https://www. youtube.com/watch?v=1q881g1L_d8, accessed August 13, 2024

2 Jennifer Cotto, "Racial Segregation Still Prevalent in Church Communities", https:// news.wttw.com/2022/08/29/racial-segregation-still-prevalent-church-communities.

church, instead of acting as if they are invisible or hoping that someone else talks to them, move towards them in the way Jesus moved towards you.

Politics

Democracy is a great gift. As citizens, we all have the right to vote for whichever politicians best coincide with our values, beliefs, and concerns. In each election cycle, we have a personal choice to make. Our vote is personal.

However, over the last few years in the US, in a way unlike at any other point in my lifetime, I've seen Christians who have appeared more devoted to their political party of choice than the call to love Jesus Christ and his people in the church.

I've heard of family members no longer talking to one another because someone in the family didn't vote a particular way in the last election. I've seen people who act appallingly toward fellow Christians because they heard that they didn't vote for the "right" candidate. Christians are longing for a political messiah to rescue them from what they feel is going wrong. Yet if we continue to allow politics to segregate, divide, and polarize us, and destroy our relationships with one another, we'll play a significant role in the marring of God's purposes and plans through his church.

So consider: Is there someone you are at odds with due to their political stance? Has your politics become your grid for how you interpret life at the expense of the Scriptures? How are you loving those around you in your church that don't agree with you politically? Has your political tribe become your comrades at the expense of brothers and sisters in Christ? How do you think God wants to deal with your heart, and stir in you love for one another in the church?

Social Media

We touched on this above, but it's worth revisiting here. We have become a "look at me" and a "like me" culture. For many of us, it's our social-media platform that has become the center of our performance. We sing, travel, eat, exercise, speak and even worship to showcase our significance to those who follow us online.

Personally, I enjoy social media—I know that I don't have to be significant on there because God is the most significant. But it's so easy to slip into unhealthy habits. It's worth asking ourselves: Are we engaging with social media for the sake of personal significance? Are we spending hours throughout the day on social media? Are we anxious about who liked or didn't like our post? Are we consumed with knowing what's happening online? If we uninstalled the app, would we be bothered? Do we struggle to take a break from scrolling? Is our heart longing for others to like us, be impressed with us, or pay attention to us?

Our longing to be the most significant person in the

room robs the people around us of our love. When we are so focused on ourselves at the expense of those around us, we miss the opportunity to stir one another up to good works, love one another, and encourage each other. We need to deal with this idol in order to love people in our church well.

LOVING ONE ANOTHER

If you're anything like me, by this point in the chapter, you're probably feeling convicted. But there's hope. In our next chapter, we'll think about how Jesus' love for us can capture our hearts and draw us away from our idols, and turn them in love towards his people.

But we must understand the seriousness of idolatry. We are commanded to worship the Lord and not turn to anything else to ultimately save or satisfy us. When we do find ourselves caught in idolatry, we must confess and repent of it. Nothing can save us but Jesus. Nothing can keep us and satisfy us but Jesus (Jeremiah 2:13; John 4:14). Significance can't save us. Money can't rescue us. Comfort can't preserve us. Idols can't win. But Jesus can and does!

Millions of people could benefit greatly from the loving witness of Christians like my grandmother and my college fraternity brother. And you can be one of those Christians, as you confess and repent of your idolatry and turn to Christ for help. Treating one another poorly isn't the way of Christ, nor his hope and plan for his bride. Instead of being harsh, may we be loving, humble, and helpful. May God help us to love one another as he loves us.

ACTION STEPS

- Write down the names of 3-5 people in your church whom you find it hard to love, or situations in which you find it difficult to be loving. Is it because you are loving an idol instead? Prayerfully consider which idols may be inhibiting your love for others within your church. (It may be one covered in this chapter, or it may be something else.)

- Seek opportunities at church this Sunday to move towards those who are from a different background than yours.

- If you think social media might be a problem for you, ask a friend or two to conduct a social-media audit with you. Over the course of a week, monitor how much you use your phone, and for what purposes, using an app such as Screen Time. Then meet up to share your results and invite each other to make observations about what you've posted. Probe your hearts, pray together, and plan steps to change.

3. LOVED BY A LOVING SAVIOR

In the previous chapter, we thought about the idols that draw us away from loving God and loving other people as we should. When we pursue significance, comfort, security, power, and money at the expense of pursuing God, it sows division among his people, causes us to overlook the needy, and harms our witness to the wider world.

So, how does God respond to his wayward, idolatrous people?

He loves.

Despite our pursuit of useless idols, God never stops pursuing his people with a relentless and steadfast love that restores and returns us to him.

It's as we grow in our appreciation of God's love that we'll grow in our ability to love and be loved by each other. We exist in Christ's body to love one another because he first loved us. Although we turn to, trust in, depend on, and give credit to idols, God knows how to destroy idols, discipline his people, and draw us back to seek after him.

GOD'S LOVE

One place where we see this is in the Old Testament book of Hosea. Hosea was prophesying right before the fall of Israel to the Assyrians. In Hosea's day, Israel had sowed unrighteousness, and pursued and worshiped idols—but God, in his grace, called them to repent.

Early in the book, God tells Hosea to marry Gomer, a woman who turns out to be very similar to the people of Israel—unfaithful! She leaves Hosea for another man and in doing so becomes a picture of the people of Israel, who have turned away from God to go after other gods. Yet Hosea is commanded by God to go and take back his unfaithful wife. Although she has sinned against him, he is to take her back and restore the relationship. This is a picture of God's love for his people.

Later in the book, in chapter 11, we get another glimpse of God's heart. No matter how unfaithful Israel is, God will never leave his covenant people. God loves, teaches, leads, and provides for Israel even though they continue sacrificing to idols, refusing to return to him, and turning away from him. Israel has proven their unfaithfulness, but the Lord is still relentless in his love for them:

> [1] *When Israel was a child, I loved him,*
>   *and out of Egypt I called my son.*
> [2] *The more they were called,*
>   *the more they went away;*
> *they kept sacrificing to the Baals*
>   *and burning offerings to idols.*

³ Yet it was I who taught Ephraim to walk;
   I took them up by their arms,
   but they did not know that I healed them.
⁴ I led them with cords of kindness,
   with the bands of love,
and I became to them as one who eases the yoke on their
jaws,
   and I bent down to them and fed them.

(Hosea 11:1-4)

Let's walk through this passage verse by verse.

In verse 1, it's as though the Lord reminisces about his relationship with Israel in the past, to make a contrast with where they are in the present. The Lord is the father, and Israel is his child: "When Israel was a child, I loved him, and out of Egypt I called my son." The Lord loves Israel and proved it when he delivered them out of slavery in Egypt.

The latter half of this verse may be familiar to you from Christmas services. Matthew's Gospel quotes it as being fulfilled in Joseph, Mary, and Jesus' escape to Egypt from the murderous hands of King Herod (Matthew 2:15). In the New Testament we see that Jesus, God's Son, is the embodiment of the true Israel. And now, by faith, we have become one with him. This means we can read these words in Hosea as true of us too. Just as the people of Israel were safely delivered out of Egypt, Jesus has delivered us out of bondage to sin. As the church, our behavior doesn't compel God's love towards us; his grace, mercy, and kindness flow to us from within himself. God loves Israel—and loves us—because of his love.

In Hosea 11:2 we're told that God further demonstrated his love by giving Israel prophets who called them to repentance. But the more they called his people to repent, the more his people rebelled; they kept sacrificing to the Baals and burning offerings to idols. The Lord sent prophets who preached and taught truth—but Israel would not turn to the truth in repentance, and instead rebelled more in the worship of their idols.

Isn't that the story of the whole Bible and of today? God pursues, and humans rebel. God pursues with love, and people rebel with idolatry. But God doesn't give up. Romans 5:6-8 says, "For while we were still weak, at the right time Christ died for the ungodly. For one will scarcely die for a righteous person—though perhaps for a good person one would dare even to die—but God shows his love for us in that while we were still sinners, Christ died for us." God's love isn't contingent on us but is given in spite of us.

Israel's rejection of God becomes even more audacious when we consider that it was God who taught Israel what they knew; they owed him everything: "It was I who taught Ephraim [another name for Israel] to walk" (Hosea 11:3), says God, like a father who teaches his child, patiently holding their hand. And as a child who falls down is scooped up by their loving father, "I took them up by their arms, but they did not know that I healed them" (v 3). Israel was taught and healed by God but gave him no credit. Instead, they gave credit to their idols.

Yet God had only ever been looking out for their good: "I led them with cords of kindness, with the bands of love, and I became to them as one who eases the yoke on their jaws, and I bent down to them and fed them" (v 4). Cords or bands were what farmers used on animals to lead them, yoking them up to train them. Then, after some time, the farmer would take the yoke off so that the animal could enjoy whatever food and water he would provide.

This is another picture of God's love and compassion for us. This isn't just what God did for Israel back then; it's what he continues to do for the church today. God lovingly teaches, heals, leads, and feeds an unfaithful people.

His love for us is relentless. He moves towards us despite our lack of movement toward him. And we can't stop God from loving us. We can't wake up one day and make God not love us. His grace pours over us. His mercy rescues us when we refuse his rescue. What grace. What mercy. What love!

GOD'S RELENTLESS LOVE

Yet one way in which parents love their children is by appropriately disciplining them. Since Israel wasn't turning back to the Lord, God declared that they would be put under a new "Pharaoh", the king of Assyria:

⁵ *They shall not return to the land of Egypt,*
  but Assyria shall be their king,
  because they have refused to return to me.
⁶ *The sword shall rage against their cities,*
  consume the bars of their gates,
  and devour them because of their own counsels.
⁷ *My people are bent on turning away from me,*
  and though they call out to the Most High,
  he shall not raise them up at all. (v 5-7)

We humans have a twisted way of thinking that we can free ourselves and save ourselves. But what we think will free us and save us—the idols of comfort, power, security, and significance—will in fact only enslave us. God had been patient with the Israelites for hundreds of years. Generation after generation, he had loved them and provided for them. But now, as a consequence of their disobedience, the sword would rage against them, consume them, and devour them—in the hands of Assyria. And this time, God would not come to their rescue (v 7). Although they would call on him in their distress and desperation, their hearts would still be turned far from him. These are sobering verses.

Yet despite this, we still see glimpses of God's grace. Notice that although Israel is unfaithful, the Lord still calls them "my people." God never disowns that which belongs to him. And what follows is probably the most emotional description of God's tenderness and compassion for his people in the Old Testament, as he wrestles and laments in his heart for Israel:

⁸ How can I give you up, O Ephraim?
  How can I hand you over, O Israel?
How can I make you like Admah?
  How can I treat you like Zeboiim?
My heart recoils within me;
  my compassion grows warm and tender.
⁹ I will not execute my burning anger;
  I will not again destroy Ephraim;
for I am God and not a man,
  the Holy One in your midst,
  and I will not come in wrath. (v 8-9)

This shows that the Lord will never completely desert his people. This is our hope amid the messiness of God's people. In our messiness, God will not desert us or turn his back; he moves towards us. Biblical history tells us that the cities of Admah and Zeboiim, mentioned in verse 8, were both annihilated along with Sodom and Gomorrah (Genesis 19:28-29; Deuteronomy 29:23). But rather than turn his people over to a similar fate, God's "compassion grows warm and tender" towards the rebellious. God could have justifiably rendered the full reality of his anger upon his people, but he chose not to.

The same is true for us. God's love comes to us in the person and work of Jesus Christ. Instead of executing his anger on us, he graciously gives us warmth. John 3:16 says, "God so loved the world, that he gave his only Son, that whoever believes in him should not perish but have eternal life." God could have given us his wrath, but instead he poured out his wrath on his Son. Unconditional love was given to rebels, and judgment was given to his Son.

If this is how God has loved us—and if this is his posture toward the brothers and sisters we gather with Sunday by Sunday—how can we not seek to love others in the same way? As the people of God, what would it look like to be consistently compassionate, tender, and warm toward one another? God's love is available for us to live out in the context of relationship with one another. As we relate to one another we could say:

Instead of giving you anger, I'm going to give you compassion!

Instead of giving you cold indifference, I choose to give you warmth and tenderness.

How can I give up on you in your sin and your struggles when God's love for you is relentless?

How can I treat you as a stranger when God has made us siblings in Christ?

God's Spirit can help us to love as God does. May God fill our hearts with this grace so that we walk out God's love among those whom we say we love. What would happen in our churches if we unconditionally loved one another with relentless love? What if we related to one another like this? What if husbands and wives and fathers and mothers and children and brothers and sisters loved and experienced love like this? What a tremendous blessing that would be within God's church.

GOD'S STEADFAST LOVE

Despite our many shortcomings, God is not finished with us. We're not at the end of the story. The people in Hosea's day weren't at the end of their story either. In Hosea 11:10-11, they're told of what would eventually happen:

> ¹⁰ *They shall go after the LORD;*
>   *he will roar like a lion;*
> *when he roars,*
>   *his children shall come trembling from the west;*
> ¹¹ *they shall come trembling like birds from Egypt,*
>   *and like doves from the land of Assyria,*
>   *and I will return them to their homes, declares the*
> *LORD. (v 10-11)*

In other words, a day of restoration would come for Israel, and they would follow the Lord. He would lead people back to where they should be. Instead of the Lord roaring with judgment and condemnation, his roar would bring his people home. They would tremble in a healthy way before him with the fear of the Lord. And unlike the silly dove who pursued foreign alliances naively, they would be like a true dove and swiftly return to their nest (v 11). This is a restoration ultimately achieved by Christ.

You might find yourself in your own metaphorical "Egypt" or in seasons of rebellion from time to time, but God can bring you back to where you belong. Not by your own doing… but because of his compassion and tender love for you. God is love, and we are loved more than we can imagine.

Take a moment and let the words of 1 John 4:10-12 wash over you: "In this is love, not that we have loved God but that he loved us and sent his Son to be the propitiation for our sins. Beloved, if God so loved us, we also ought to love one another. No one has ever seen God; if we love one another, God abides in us and his love is perfected in us." God loved us despite our poor choices, disobedience, and turning away from his truth. He proved it by sending his own sinless Son, who became sin for us. His love is real. This is why we can love one another. Jesus first loved us: so much so that he gave his life. How can we not love one another? How can we not extend grace to one another? "We love because he first loved us" (v 19).

In Romans 8:37-39, Paul shares his concluding reflection on chapters 5 – 8 when he says:

> In all these things we are more than conquerors through him who loved us. For I am sure that neither death nor life, nor angels nor rulers, nor things present nor things to come, nor powers, nor height nor depth, nor anything else in all creation, will be able to separate us from the love of God in Christ Jesus our Lord.

In the preceding verses, Paul reminds us that God is for us (v 31-34). How is he for us? God is for us in giving us his Son, who guarantees and secures our ability to move through this life in love until we attain our final salvation. This means that no one can bring a consequential charge against us that will stand before God. We are in a far better position than the Israelites were!

Perhaps reading this chapter has caused you to feel deeply convicted by your lack of love for others. Take heart: it is God who has chosen us and justified us, and it his Son who defends us and answers any charge brought against us. We can't be separated from this love. Nothing can tear us from God or his love towards us. Nothing on this earth can destroy this relationship. Nor can any spiritual power separate us from God's love. God's love for us through Christ reigns over our lives and will never cease. He will bring you home to stand before him in glorious perfection.

What is trying to convince you otherwise? What is seeking to persuade you into believing that this isn't true for you? Never forget—God loves you. His love is relentless towards you. His love will never cease for you. Jesus is devoted to you.

And he's devoted to your brothers and sisters in Christ. You are all empowered to love one another with this love. This means that the people who you do life with and see every Sunday are precious people for whom Christ died. They are to be recipients of this love. When we see people as God sees them, we will seek to love them as God loves them.

ACTION STEPS

- Choose one verse from Hosea 11 that has particularly struck you and spend time meditating on it.

- Keep coming back to the verse throughout the week to remind yourself of God's love for you. You could write it out and put it up somewhere that you'll see it, set it as your phone screen, commit it to memory—or something else!

4. ONE-ANOTHERING IN ACTION

One of the hardest seasons of my life was when—after several years of severe neurological issues—my wife, Leslie, was told that she had to have brain surgery. We were simultaneously devastated and hopeful. We knew that if she didn't have the surgery, things could get much worse than they were. But there would be significant risks and a long recovery.

At first, we weren't sure whether to speak publicly at church about the need for surgery and the subsequent conditions. But in the event, we chose to share; we chose to let our church be our family.

It was the best decision we could have made. The church loved us so well. People were constantly praying for us. The elders laid hands on Leslie, asking God to heal her and to empower the surgeon—who, by God's grace, was one of the best surgeons in the country for my wife's specific issues. On the day of the surgery, church members took Leslie's mom out for lunch, which helped her break up the long hours in the hospital waiting room.

Once Leslie was sent home, our church family prepared meals for us. They cleaned our house and took turns spending time with Leslie as I returned to work after several weeks. The elders preached for me to lighten the load. They loved us like family. We never regret letting them be family—because, in the end, one of the hardest seasons of our life became one of the most beautiful.

THE TEXTURE OF THE CHRISTIAN LIFE

I share that to give you a picture of the New Testament's "one-another commands" in action. Author and pastor John Piper explains what that means: "Around fifty times in the New Testament, Jesus and the apostles tell us to feel, say, or do something to 'one another.' We are to care for one another and bear with one another, honor one another and sing to one another, do good to one another and forgive one another."[3]

The one-anothers in Scripture offer us a beautiful picture of life together in community under the lordship of Jesus Christ. They are all given within the context of the local church for the glory of God. They show us how God's people, gathered around God's name, grow in unity and relationship. One-anothering brings texture to our call to live like Christ-followers. They move us from love in

---

3 https://www.desiringgod.org/articles/the-art-of-one-anothering (accessed August 14, 2023).

theory to love in practice. And every one-another Jesus did perfectly himself on earth—so he's never asking us to do something he himself didn't accomplish or which he cannot empower us to do too.

In this chapter, we'll consider a handful of these one-another commands.

LOVE ONE ANOTHER

And above all these put on love, which binds everything together in perfect harmony. (Colossians 3:14)

Of the 59 or so one-anothers in the Bible, the command to love another is the most repeated. It's also the most foundational. It's what binds all the other qualities "together in perfect harmony." It's the linchpin of Christ-like relationships.

So, what are we talking about when we say "love"? We're talking about the selfless, sacrificial giving of oneself for the sake of someone else. 1 Corinthians 13:4-5 says, "Love is patient and kind; love does not envy or boast; it is not arrogant or rude. It does not insist on its own way; it is not irritable or resentful." Since Jesus loves us, we are called to love one another. He calls us to love one another with unconditional love.

Loving one another in the church means listening to the needs of people in the church and asking God to help you meet them. It may include offering people car rides (even when inconvenient), making meals for expectant moms, cutting someone's grass, cleaning someone's house, letting them borrow your car, and sitting with people in the hospital or at home when they're ill or infirm.

Less tangibly—but no less importantly—we love by listening to one another without always being quick to give our opinions. Love means not being rude or dismissive to one another in conversations—even the ones that feel long and drawn out. Don't cut people off mid-sentence or try to outdo someone's story with your "better" story. Loving one another says, *No matter how irritating I might find you, I will seek your best interests!*

SERVE ONE ANOTHER

For you were called to freedom, brothers. Only do not use your freedom as an opportunity for the flesh, but through love serve one another. For the whole law is fulfilled in one word: You shall love your neighbor as yourself. (Galatians 5:13-14)

Jesus Christ served us through the gospel. Since he did that, we can serve one another. In our flesh—our sinful nature—we want to be served rather than to serve. But when we depend on God's grace, he allows us, through love, to serve one another (v 13-14).

Christ purchased our freedom on the cross. Our freedom isn't a freedom *from* service, but a freedom *for* service. Apart from grace, all our "serving" is self-serving in some capacity. But because of grace, we're free to serve one another through love. We're not trying to prove ourselves anymore or advance our own agenda. We are simply serving one another.

Where are you in your service of brothers and sisters in the church in the following areas?

- *Serving others, not self, with your money.* We all have plenty of things we can think of doing with our money. But serving others, not self, means being willing to use it for another's sake. If you hear of those in a season of financial challenge or distress, you could buy them a gift card for a grocery store. If you come across someone in your community group who needs help with their bills, you could ask your community-group leader if it's fitting for you to contribute. If someone needs a car, you could help them find one and consider donating to the purchase cost.

- *Serving others, not self, with your words.* Some of us get awkward about giving encouragement. We feel embarrassed any time we try to say something from the heart. But serving others with our words means using them to encourage others, even if it makes us feel vulnerable. But if you struggle with that, why not try written encouragement? Writing anything is rare these days. But a handwritten note of encouragement goes a long way. You can serve someone by telling them how much of a gift they are to you. Point out unique attributes in them that you enjoy and are blessed by. Or remember someone's birthday or anniversary with a written card. If someone appears downcast or sad, you could send them a note letting them know you're praying for them and available if they need anything.

- *Serving others, not self, with your time.* Some of us are cash rich but time poor. There's so much we want to get done. But would you be willing to drop your to-do list and put your time at another person's disposal? You can serve people by reminding them that you are here for them— especially when things are difficult. When you're going through hard times, the person who sticks out the most is the one that presses in and makes themselves available to support you.

- *Serving others, not self, with your gifts.* "As each has received a gift, use it to serve one another, as good stewards of God's varied grace" (1 Peter 4:10). If you're a believer, you've been endowed with a spiritual gift to build up God's church! For example, if we have the gift of giving, we use our gift to meet the tangible needs of others in the body. If we have the spiritual gift of faith, we help to strengthen the hearts of others around us to trust in the goodness of God. If we have the gift of mercy, we show compassion to those who need God's mercy. If we have the gift of administration, we seek opportunities to organize church life in a way that brings blessing to others.

It's easy to make using our gifts all about us. Too often, what we really want is to make ourselves look good. But the gospel teaches us that it's about looking out, not looking good. In whatever way God has gifted you, use what grace has provided to look out for those around you.

HONOR ONE ANOTHER

Love one another with brotherly affection. Outdo one another in showing honor. (Romans 12:10)

The world's version of honoring one another is based on reciprocity. Society says, "I'll honor you if you honor me. I'll respect you if you do the same for me. If you give good energy, I'll give you good energy back." However, the Bible teaches us to seek to outdo one another in showing honor. However much (or however little) honor people show us, we seek to show them more. Don't let what you perceive to be someone's lack of respect for you affect how you treat them. As an Olympic athlete seeks to outdo his or her opponents, we, as Christians, must go out of our way to honor one another.

How do we outdo one another in showing honor? There are two areas where this can be particularly hard.

- Recognize every person as a person. I'm thinking here particularly about someone whom you wouldn't naturally consider to be your friend: those who are somehow different from you or who are outside your normal social circle. Regardless of your relationship with someone, demonstrate honor when speaking with them with eye contact, listening with interest to what they are saying, and going out of your way to be respectful. When we pay attention to people, we demonstrate that they matter. That attention communicates to the person, "I see you, and I respect you." We must learn to recognize and appreciate those around us.

- Be honorable in disagreements. Typically, disagreements are viewed as a time to speak your mind and prove your point, however callously. But there is no place for harsh words or personal put-downs in the church. Sometimes, outdoing one another in showing honor means surrendering the need to win the argument. Seek to win your friend, not the argument, by staying respectful.

Simply put, the church is a place where honoring should be happening all the time.

BUILD ONE ANOTHER UP

Therefore encourage one another and build one another up, just as you are doing. (1 Thessalonians 5:11)

In 2018, our church refitted an old adult daycare center and turned it into a place for us to meet. It began with a dream. Then came a design plan, layout, and architectural drawings. Next we had to seek city approvals and hire a contractor, who gathered the materials to get it going. The whole process was intentional and thoroughly thought out. We started the project with a desire for what we wanted it to become. We didn't build without vision.

The same is true of the church on a spiritual level. Jesus is the builder of his church. He's the one with the vision, and we join him by playing the part to which he's called us.

That means building one another up. We are called to edify and strengthen one another—to help one another to grow in our faith and character, by reminding each other of what God has said and what he is doing.

Paul celebrated the witness of the Thessalonian church and encouraged them to keep after it: *Never stop building one another up. Keep it at the forefront of everything that you do.* But here's the challenge for us. We struggle to build one another up because we love building up and looking out for ourselves. But through Christ, we can intentionally edify and strengthen one another.

So let's build! How do we practically build one another up?

- Use your words to edify people. Using hurtful language and coarse jesting doesn't build up; it tears down. When talking to one another, be mindful of what you're saying. Say things like, "Every time I see you, I get inspired to be thoughtful like you." "I appreciate you for how you love your spouse and children." Words matter. Words can be encouraging or destructive.

- Notice people using their spiritual gifts. Pay attention to how your brothers and sisters trust God with their spiritual gifts. If you see someone deliberately exercising their gift, let them know how it's impacting you. Remind them that God has uniquely gifted them, and let them know that they are stewarding their gifts well. Often people get discouraged in ministry. So build them up!

- Seek to restore the fallen believer. Sometimes the church can be quick to deal with sin but slow to build up the contrite sinner. When people fall, their shame weighs heavily on their hearts. However, if a fallen Christian is remorseful or repentant, be someone who reminds them that although they have sinned, they can be loved again. They are not forgotten. They are not irredeemably damaged goods. Tell people that. For example, tell the repentant adulterer that you are available to walk with them to restoration as a member of Christ's body. Remind them of God's thoughts about them. Remind them that Jesus is still on the throne. Dream with them of a hope-filled future. See what they can't see about themselves and tell them. Build one another up!

CHRIST'S LOVE ON DISPLAY

My hope as a pastor is to lead my church in living out the one-anothers so that each member will be shaped by the love of Christ on display through his people—just as my wife and I were when Leslie had surgery. As a leadership team, we're trying to create more spaces for people to one-another. Whether through Sunday morning gatherings, midweek small groups that we call gospel communities, or special events for men, women, and students, we are putting in place pathways for practical one-anothering. By God's grace, we are seeing more of it happening. It's such a joy for me as a pastor to see people of all ages love, serve, and build up one another.

A surprising space where people live out the one-anothers is our community vegetable garden behind our church building. We created this project to bring people from our neighborhood together to work alongside and experience the love of Christ's people. We hoped that as people saw Christians interacting with one another, they'd be struck by the quality of our relationships. By God's grace, it's been a real success. The desire of our church is that our collective one-anothering will continue to serve as a magnet for newcomers. We hope that the fresh fruit and vegetables we grow will nourish bodies and also blow the fragrant aroma of Christ into the hearts and lives of those without Jesus. To God be the glory.

ACTION STEPS

- Write a note of encouragement to a fellow church member: perhaps someone who has inspired you personally by the way they use their gifts; or someone who seems particularly weary.

- Consider whether there is someone in your church with a particular need of some kind, and how you could seek to meet it.

- Are you using your gifts to build up the body? If not, talk to your church leaders about ways to get involved. If you're not sure what your gifts are, ask a Christian friend what they think.

- This Sunday, seek to:
  1. Practice honoring others by giving at least one person more of your attention than you would otherwise have done.
  2. Intentionally express your appreciation of at least one person for whom you wouldn't normally do this.

5. UNCONDITIONAL LOVE
IN A DIVIDED CULTURE

Before I planted my current church, I taught counseling at a seminary in Washington, D.C. Looking around the classroom, it often felt like the United Nations! The seminary drew all kinds of people who looked, loved, and lived differently than me. People who were African American, White, Latino, Asian, African, Hispanic, and those from various people groups from the Caribbean islands were all part of the classes. The counseling program invited (forced!) me, the teacher, to step into the shoes of others and learn from their experiences.

God used one class in particular to shape my vision for future ministry. This class was a melting pot of aspiring Christian counselors who built a bond for 16 intimate weeks. We truly cared for each other: we hugged, cried, walked through confusion, confessed sin, and laughed together. And what was the result of that? It changed my life. That we had all seen each other's biases, scars, and flaws and *still* chose to walk with one another in love did something within my heart. Simply put, it expanded the scope of what I understood it to mean to unconditionally love a diverse group of people.

This was the impetus for the Lord's calling on my life to start Wellspring Church in North Carolina. I began to think, "Why can this experience of unconditional love and acceptance only happen in the classroom and not the church?" I hoped that there could be a way for people who, on the surface, have no business being in the same room together to walk patiently with each other through the ups and downs of life.

You see, the church at large likes to say that we love one another unconditionally. But time and time again, our cultural context challenges the outworking of that love. It may be an election season when there's disagreement about who to vote for; or differing views on how to best work out the ethic of the gospel in social spaces; or the temptation to "cancel" people who don't view every secondary issue in the same way as you. It quickly becomes evident that our "unconditional love" isn't so unconditional.

So, as I prepared to plant Wellspring Church, I began a journey of seeking the Lord, asking, "How can we be a church that is united in love—when culture, history, and personal life experiences have the potential to divide us around every issue?" That's the question we're going to consider in this chapter.

UNCONDITIONAL LOVE: VERTICAL

A key text on church unity is Ephesians 2. Here the author, Paul, starts not with the "horizontal" division between Jews and non-Jews (Gentiles) but with the "vertical" reconciliation that has taken place between the believer and God. He tells his non-Jewish readers:

> *Remember that you were at that time separated from Christ, alienated from the commonwealth of Israel and strangers to the covenants of promise, having no hope and without God in the world. But now in Christ Jesus you who once were far off have been brought near by the blood of Christ. (v 12-13)*

One glorious implication of the gospel is that Gentiles—those far away from God, who were not included in the covenant promises he made to the Israelites—have now been brought near to God by the blood of Christ.

Jesus' blood shed for guilty sinners is the epitome of unconditional love—he died for us while we were still sinners (Romans 5:8). Think about that. You didn't have to eradicate your sin problem for God to love you. God, in his mercy and grace, unconditionally chooses (or elects) those that he saves, without respect to any conditions being met on our part. He doesn't say, *I'll save Dwayne, so long as he never sins again, or so long as he meets me halfway with good deeds, or so long as he has a perfect understanding of me.* No—God's election of me, and of you, is unconditional. There's nothing that I've done or anything in me that warrants his love. Quite the opposite. As the author Tim Keller put it, "God doesn't just love you unconditionally. He loves you counter-conditionally—in spite of your conditions."[4] Unconditional love, then, is the enduring commitment to the good of another regardless of how deserving or undeserving that person is.

We'll only be able to extend unconditional love "horizontally" to our brothers and sisters if we have first experienced the "vertical" unconditional love of God. We who were once God's enemies have now become sons and siblings through Jesus' death, burial, and resurrection. We have peace with God and access to his grace (Romans 5:1-2). We are his people forever. Because of Jesus, we now live face to face with God.

UNCONDITIONAL LOVE: HORIZONTAL

Living face to face with God means we can also live face to face with one another. As God's friend, I can love people around me in the way that God loves me. I can choose to love people not because they are lovely but because God chose me when I was unlovable.

That's what Paul says next in Ephesians 2:

For [Christ] himself is our peace, who has made us both one and has broken down in his flesh the dividing wall of hostility by abolishing the law of commandments

---

4 Timothy Keller, "Does God Control Everything?" https://gospelinlife.com/sermon/does-god-control-everything/ (accessed August 9, 2024).

expressed in ordinances, that he might create in himself
one new man in place of the two, so making peace, and
might reconcile us both to God in one body through the
cross, thereby killing the hostility. (v 14-16)

Christ defeats the hostility between divided groups. He broke down the dividing wall of hostility between Jews and Gentiles. In the temple in Jerusalem, there was a literal wall—a barrier separating the outer Court of the Gentiles from the inner parts of the temple where only Jewish people could go. Historically, this was a status line that kept the Jews closest to God and the Gentile participants worshiping from a distance. This led to Jews feeling superior because they were "closest" to God. They thought they were better because of their pedigree, ethnicity, education, and spiritual heritage. They didn't associate with Gentiles.

But Paul says that's not how it's to be in the church, which was made up of both Jewish and Gentile believers. Since both Jews and Gentiles need their vertical relationship with God to be established wholly upon the merit of Jesus Christ, and not their good works, none can boast (v 9). The logic of the gospel says that those who would boast in their works can no longer boast, for works can't save. Those who would boast in their ethnicity can no longer boast, for ethnicity doesn't give them privilege with God. Those who would boast in their education cannot boast, for God doesn't take that into account. The things the Jews had leveraged against the Gentiles had no value at the foot of the cross. Both Jews and Gentiles shared the same need, and they shared the same salvation. There was no place for hostility between them.

The same is true today. There is no place for hostility between Christians who vote Republican and Christians who vote Democrat, for political affiliation gives you no upper hand with God. There is no place for disparaging language from Christians who "just preach the gospel" against Christians who believe the gospel leads them to push for policy change. And vice versa. Paul is saying that hostility doesn't make any sense because, in God's eyes, there's no currency with which you can elevate yourself against others. Your leverage for separation or superiority, whatever it may be, means nothing for salvation.

The cross has brought together disparate people who were once separated by ethnicity, culture, nationality, upbringing, or economic and social status. God's unconditional love has united us, making us one; he has created "in himself one new man in place of the two" (v 15). We are now united with Christ, which unites us to all of God's people—the church.

HOW A DIVIDED CULTURE TRIES TO DEFEAT UNCONDITIONAL LOVE

All that is true. But it's hard to live out. A culture divided by so many things—race, politics, economics, education and more—seeks to hinder Christians from loving one another unconditionally.

For instance, one way that our divided culture teaches us to "love" is based on reciprocity. In other words, we tend to extend love to those who benefit us in some way. We relate to people based on their status, prestige, power, or position of influence, or whether they can love us back. In her novel *The Sea of Tranquility*, Katja Millay says, "People like to say love is unconditional, but it's not, and even if it was unconditional, it's still never free. There's always an expectation attached. They always want something in return."[5]

Ask yourself: Do you find yourself avoiding certain people in conversation before or after a Sunday service because deep down, you don't want to be seen caught up in a conversation with "that kind of person"? Do you gravitate towards those who are in the "inner ring" of church life, socially speaking? Do you ever find yourself serving because, deep down, you think others will be impressed by your sacrificial heart? Or because the person you serve might feel they owe you one, which could come in handy?

Another way that our divided culture teaches us to "love" is based on uniformity. We only love those who agree with us. We knowingly or unknowingly say to ourselves, "If you're on my side, you're in. If you aren't on my side, then you're out." This makes love something that is earned rather than something that is unconditionally extended to all.

---

5 Katja Millay, *The Sea of Tranquility: A Novel* (Atria Books, 2013), p. 227.

Ask yourself: Are there people you invite to dinner at your home because you like them and agree with them on most things—so you know you won't have to debate with them on issues of politics or parenting or the environment or whatever else is contentious? Conversely, are there people you *don't* invite because you know you don't want to have those discussions?

Connected to uniformity, there's a cancel culture. This way of relating to others leaves no room for nuance. It says, "If you're with me, I need 100% of your affirmation. Anything less will result in 100% cancellation." Cancel culture is unequivocally desirous of a total ideological commitment.

The church is not exempt here, either. Though it may not be termed "cancel culture," many churches (even those who "just care about the gospel") insist on ideologies extending far beyond the gospel. So consider: Do the majority of members at your church think the same way about politics? Do the majority educate their children in the same way and secretly disparage those that choose a different route? That could be a sign of ill-health. Christians who relate on the basis of uniformity miss the opportunity, and privilege, to live out vertical and horizontal unconditional love among the diverse body of Christ.

If we insist that others either reciprocate or conform before we love them, it subtly puts a "cost" of being accepted on others when the blood of Jesus demands that you accept them freely out of unconditional love. Instead of God being at the center of our responses to one another, we are at the center. We negate the truth that God's love has been extended to us freely, but at great cost to him.

In Galatians 2:11-14, we read of how Paul confronted Peter for relating to Gentile Christians with an attitude of sinful discrimination. The Gentiles hurt Peter's status in the eyes of the Jews, so he didn't eat with them. Paul said that this was out of step with the unconditional love of God in the gospel. But Paul didn't cancel Peter; he reminded him of the gospel truth. Let's be those who do likewise.

FIVE DYNAMICS OF UNCONDITIONAL LOVE IN A DIVIDED CULTURE

So where do we go from here? How do we live a life of unconditional love in a divided culture? Well, I have five dynamics to suggest.

1. Fuel Your Horizontal Love out of God's Unconditional Vertical Love

I remember when I first met Dr. K. He was the chairman of a counseling program; I was a prospective student. He was humble, kindhearted, thoughtful, understanding, and intuitive, and a great listener. As I met with him to determine whether I would enroll in his counseling program, I shared my story with him. As I did, it became clear that regardless of whether I enrolled in the program, he cared about me. After our meeting, I hurried home to my wife and shared parts of the conversation. After a season of prayer and additional conversations with my wife, I quit my lucrative job as a sales executive in a technology company and enrolled in the program.

As I began to take classes, it became even more apparent that he genuinely cared for me, not just as a student but also as a person. In our one-on-one counseling labs, raw truth about my ugly past, my feelings of injustice as an African American man, and broken stories of relational failure didn't push him away. It didn't turn him away from me. Instead, it turned him toward me. Nothing I shared with him caused him to love and care for me differently. I was grateful to be fully known and fully loved. Outside of my marriage relationship with my beautiful wife, this was one of my few experiences of being fully known and unconditionally loved. My heart was gently cracked open to understand that this was but a small glimpse of God's all-knowing, unconditional love for me. I'd never experienced God's love before in the way that I did during that season. It was life-changing.

This revitalized understanding of God's love for me fueled my love of others and my desire to help them experience the unconditional love of God for themselves through counseling. Since I graduated in 2001, I have counseled hundreds of people who are ethnically, culturally, and socially different from me. They don't look like me.

They weren't raised like me. They were simply in need of unconditional love.

The people in your life need the very same thing. And the only way that we can find the fuel to give this kind of love is by receiving it from God. We need to fill up on God's unconditional love every day by spending time with him in his word, meditating on his love for us.

2. Commit to Forgiving Others as You've Been Forgiven in Christ

Just as Jesus' unconditional love for us fuels our love for others, so too the forgiveness that we've received in Christ empowers us to forgive.

That doesn't make it easy. "But what about when I'm hurt by people who are supposed to love me?" you might be thinking. I've been there. "What about when a fellow church member abandons our relationship without notice? I've been there for them. I've cried with them. I've mutually confided in them. I've spent countless hours pouring my life into them—for what? The person that I've loved now ghosts me, ignores my texts, leaves without saying goodbye, deserts our friendship, and acts as if they never were in a relationship with me. What do I do with this? How do I respond?"

I commit to forgiving them as I've been forgiven in Christ. When I was ghosting, ignoring, and deserting Christ—completely unconcerned about him—he pursued me and chose me. So, even if I don't like what someone has done to hurt me, I can prayerfully seek to forgive them because Christ similarly loved me.

Does this mean that I need to reinvest in the friendship? Not necessarily. But it means I can love them because I've been loved in Christ without conditions. And if they do repent and ask for forgiveness, by the power of the Spirit I may indeed reinvest.

Even if they don't come to seek restoration with me, I can, by God's grace, take the cost of the offense that they've imposed on me and place it on Christ's shoulders. I can ask God to keep my heart tender and not bitter towards them. I can long for reconciliation and pray for them to that end. In the Spirit's power, I can resist the temptation to badmouth them to my current friends. This is what forgiveness looks like.

3. Count the Cost of Unconditional Love

In our church, we have what we call gospel community groups, which come together during the week to do life together. Everyone is invited to participate in a group. No one is excluded. We've intentionally formed them based on location rather than any other factor so that people can't choose what group they are in. It's based on geography.

As these groups of ethnically, culturally, and sociologically diverse people come together week by week, there are plenty of opportunities for loving one another unconditionally! When things go wrong or get tense, or when feelings get hurt or relationships go awry, we hang in there and trust God's work in us through the gospel to give us what we need for one another. In signing up for the groups, we agree to press into the mess rather than run away. This is the cost of unconditional love.

You too are called to count the cost of unconditional love as you do life in your community. This looks like pressing into the mess, weirdness, and relational complexities within your Christian community even when it's costly. For example, when you don't agree with a fellow church member, you choose to love them instead of trying to find a new church. Or, if you don't agree with your church leaders, you choose to love them instead of venting to fellow members and stirring up dissension. You talk through disagreements, and you bear with one another in love. Christ invites us into the mess with him.

4. View Everyone as Image-Bearers Worthy of Dignity

In a divided culture, it's easy to see people according to their outward appearance, status, ethnicity, position, net worth, pedigree, or even what they've done or not done for you. We must be reminded, however, that regardless of all that, people are created in the image and likeness of God (Genesis 1:26-27). People don't earn dignity; they possess dignity as image-bearers. Sin mars God's image in us, but it doesn't strip us of that inherent dignity. Therefore, Christ's body must treat people with dignity; we must view people as image-bearers in need of unconditional love and acceptance. One blogger said it like this: "Unconditional love does not mean that God loves everything we do, but rather His love is so intense that He loves every sinner, no matter how vile and despicable he or she may be in the eyes of humanity, so much that He provides a way for them to find love, life, and holiness."[6]

What does this look like? It looks like engaging with people despite their behavior, attitudes, moods, edgy personality, or poor relational responses. Picture the person in church that you avoid the most. Viewing them as an image-bearer worthy of dignity means choosing to engage with, care for, and genuinely invest in their personal wellbeing.

5. Have Realistic Relational Expectations

We must be realistic. Loving broken people is hard. Saying all the right things all the time is impossible. Never experiencing relational tension with people is almost impossible. As redeemed sinners, we trust God to be at work in us. But we are mere men and women and not the Messiah. We must accept that we will get it wrong, and that other people will get it wrong too.

---

6 R. Keith Whitt, "What does it mean that God's love is unconditional?" https://www.biblestudytools.com/bible-study/topical-studies/the-unconditional-love-of-god.html (accessed August 9, 2024).

We will be misunderstood, offended, misconstrued, misrepresented, and so on. You will encounter division and difficulty even when trying to mend divisions!

When that happens, return again to the assurances of God's vertical love to live horizontally among those around you. The Pastor and author Dr. Paul Tripp asks, "Are you looking for love horizontally when it can only be found vertically? Are you asking an imperfect person to love you unconditionally in a way that your Heavenly Father can only supply? How will that unrealistic pressure put a strain on this relationship?"[7] But if we have realistic expectations of one another in the church, we'll be enabled to persevere in the power of the Spirit—coming back again and again to the fountain of love, the Lord Jesus.

GOD'S LOVE ON DISPLAY

As we love one another, God's church becomes the city on a hill that exudes Christ's unconditional love. We become a unified house full of people whose only allegiance is to him, his kingdom, and his people—undivided by race, ethnicity, socioeconomics, and politics. A place where sinful, broken, scarred, and needy people can meet Jesus and grow in grace.

Sometimes I think, "If my church could only have seen what I saw in my seminary class over two decades ago,

---

7 Paul Tripp, "True and Perfect Love," https://www.paultripp.com/wednesdays-word/posts/true-and-perfect-love (accessed August 9, 2024).

they too would catch the vision." But then I remember that we have a better display than my seminary class that they can look to—we have the unconditional love of the sinless Savior, giving his life for us and making us one in him. Looking to him, I hope all the more in what God is doing.

ACTION STEPS

- Write a list of your meaningful church relationships and consider how many of these are based on reciprocity or uniformity. Prayerfully identify one person who is different from you with whom you could seek to forge a deeper friendship.

- Reflect on whether there is someone in your church family whom you need to forgive, and what this would look like. Talk this through with a trusted Christian friend.

6. WHEN MULTIETHNIC CHURCH BECOMES A LOVING FAMILY

My city of Charlotte, North Carolina, is home to NFL team Carolina Panthers. Their games are a crazy gathering of all types of people. On game day, the nearly 75,000 people at Bank of America Stadium comprise all races and faces: men, women, and children; African-American, Latino, and White people—all dressed in Carolina blue-and-white. It's a sight to behold.

We're a diverse crowd cheering on a diverse team with diverse skills—offense, defense, and coaches. When we gather, we're going after the one goal—to win the game. And yet, after the game ends, we all go our separate ways, back to our separate lives. We're not really friends, let alone family.

Church can be like this sometimes. We might be blessed enough to gather in a multiethnic group on Sunday, but at the end of the service, we simply say amen, walk out, and return to our comfort zones. Sadly though, our comfort zone is often our color zone.

We've touched on the area of racial diversity and unity at several points in this book so far. In this chapter, though, I want us to give it our full attention. How can a multiethnic church become a loving family? What does it look like to care for one another across ethnic difference?

DEFINING TERMS

We need to make two definitions clear from the beginning. First, what is a "multiethnic" church? Second, what do we mean by a "loving family"? We must understand what it is we're aiming for before we begin to talk about the solution.

- *Multiethnic church:* "A church in which there is 1) an attitude and practice of accepting people of all ethnic, class and national origins as equal and fully participating members and ministers in the fellowship of the church; and 2) the manifestation of this attitude and practice by the involvement of people from different ethnic, social and national communities as members in the church."[8] As we saw from Ephesians in the previous chapter, the New Testament leads us to expect people from all kinds of backgrounds to respond to the good news; and that good news makes us one body (Ephesians 2:14-16).

---

8 Gary McIntosh, "Defining a Multi-ethnic Church," The Food Book Blog, Talbot School of Theology Faculty blog (April 24, 2012); https://www.biola.edu/blogs/good-book-blog/2012/defining-a-multi-ethnic-church (accessed July 6, 2023).

- *Loving family:* A loving family is a group of people who, regardless of biological connection, are devoted to one another in love, care, commitment, presence, provision, dependence, and trust.

The problem, however, is that many churches fall into one of two spaces:

1. We Experience Loving Family but Are Not Multiethnic

There are some churches where God's love is expressed in real and evident ways. People are serving one another, being kind, supportive, encouraging, and sacrificial. Yet, when you survey the look and feel of those gathered, you quickly see that they are culturally homogenous. As previously mentioned, back in the 1960s, the civil rights campaigner Martin Luther King, Jr. said, "It is one of the tragedies of our nation ... that eleven o'clock on Sunday morning is one of the most segregated hours ... in Christian America."[9] Sadly, this is still the case in America today.

Granted, some churches exist in areas that are relatively culturally homogeneous. When this is the case, it's unsurprising that a Sunday morning doesn't feel that diverse. If that's your context, it's still worth considering: if a Christian who looked different from the predominant

---

9 "The Most Segregated Hour in America - Martin Luther King Jr"; https://www. youtube.com/watch?v=1q881g1L_d8 (accessed August 13, 2024).

population came, would they be welcomed and loved as part of the family?

I suspect that most people reading this, however, live in a more diverse area. If that's you, has your church settled for homogeneity? Can your church family be considered truly loving if the diversity of God's people in your local community isn't welcomed?

2. We Experience a Multiethnic Church Gathering, Yet We Are Still Not a Loving Family

A bit like the Panthers stadium, it's possible to be a diverse church but not do life like a family. Diverse people of all types can be present without love. Many churches *look* like heaven on the surface without *loving* like heaven underneath. The true outworking of the gospel is a multiethnic church that beautifully displays the love of God among its people.

We see that on the day of Pentecost. When the power of the Holy Spirit showed up in Acts 2, it enabled a diverse group of Jewish people "from every nation under heaven" to assemble and hear about the mighty works of God in their own language (v 5, 9-11). Then Peter stood with the other eleven apostles and preached a robust gospel message (v 14-36). Their hearers responded with repentance and faith (v 37-41). This diverse crowd was now the family of God, brought together by the sovereign will of God and the power of the Holy Spirit.

In the very next verses, we read how this loving family devoted themselves to the apostles' teaching and to one another. They ate together "in their homes" (v 46). They cared for one another by "selling their possessions and belongings and distributing the proceeds to all, as any had need" (v 45). At the heart of their devotion was love. This was family in action.

An important thing to remember is that you don't "arrive" at being a multiethnic, loving family. You're constantly battling for it. What is needed is a Holy Spirit-powered commitment to enduring unity. There will be many barriers to being a devoted Acts-2-style church. Let's consider some of them.

BARRIERS TO BECOMING A LOVING FAMILY

It doesn't take too much to see that, in their own power, churches just don't seem to have what it takes to become a diverse, loving family. The hearts of humans often attempt to stall the purposes of God. Therefore, it takes great intentionality to foster a diverse and loving dynamic in a church. Here are just some of the things that often hinder it.

1. One Group's Cultural Preferences Get Elevated above Another's

So much of what we do when we gather for worship as a church comes down to preference—and so much of preference comes down to culture.

For example, there's music. What kind of music would be common in a multi-ethnic church? Is it hymns or "gospel music," modern or traditional? What instruments should we play? Majority White culture and ethnic minority groups have developed different musical traditions and desires when it comes to sung worship. But to be a loving family, "let each of you look not only to his own interests, but also to the interests of others" (Philippians 2:4).

Second, there's the question of emotional expression in public worship. Ethnic minorities, particularly African Americans, are traditionally more emotionally expressive in worship. Shouts, hand claps, swaying, verbal "amens," and so on have all been a part of the African American history of struggle in America. In my ministry experience, I've noticed that often my White brothers and sisters are more accustomed to worship that prioritizes what they call the contemplative or intellectual side of singing. They may be hesitant about emotional expression out of a fear of inauthenticity—they don't want to clap and raise their hands and shout unless they truly "feel it."

In a church family that has people coming from both of these backgrounds, how do you proceed when emotional expression is essential to the heart and soul of half your congregation, while it is a distraction to the contemplative mind of the other half? How does a church create a culture where emotional expression is practiced in a way that fosters love in the community?

That will very much depend on your context; but let's keep love at the center. Let's lovingly allow each other to express ourselves as the Holy Spirit leads and learn from one another. Let's allow people to be different than us and still be a part of the loving family of God.

Third, there's community. How do distinct ethnicities and cultures experience church community? Historically, the African American church does community through having its people attend Sunday morning worship. We learn through hearing the word and participating in worship together. Centralized Bible study and discipleship classes are common, and as relationships develop organically, that leads to people to spending other time together as well. White churches do these things too, but in addition they'll often emphasize the importance of midweek small groups in peoples' homes (whether they go by the name of community groups, life groups, gospel communities, or something else.)

When both cultures exist alongside each other in a multiethnic church, it's important that one cultural preference isn't pursued and normalized without first understanding the dynamics of the other cultures present. To be a loving family, the leaders must assess the needs of those present and prayerfully move toward a model that they judge will best facilitate a loving opportunity among their congregation.

2. We Desire Multi-Ethnicity Because of the Cultural Climate Rather than Theological Conviction

The multiethnic church isn't a new thing. It isn't a response to the cultural pressure of our day or the need to resolve race relations in the 21st century; its origins are in the gospel (Acts 2; Acts 13; Ephesians 2 – 3). Frankly, when the motivation for growing a multiethnic church is due to anything other than the Scriptures, we risk acting from a place of pragmatism instead of theological conviction. Trying to remediate race issues with multiethnicity apart from gospel love can quickly become tokenism. It may result in mere "trophy" churches. These churches are multiethnic visually without being a loving church at the core. Instead, we need loving multiethnic churches that are lead with theological convictions.

3. We Fail to Realize That People Have Different Experiences That Often Shape How They Interpret Life

People are unique. Every ethnic group and culture interprets life through their own grid, which shapes how we engage with those around us. When a multiethnic church seeks to gather together as a loving church, we must admit that such preferences and biases exist. However, that doesn't have to imply anything wrong. It just means that each person possesses a way of interpreting life that could impact how we develop as a loving family.

To help that process, we must each give grace to one another and believe the best of one another, even if we don't understand each other. Just because you didn't grow up a certain way doesn't mean that it's wrong. Not all biases are harmful, but they do all need to be checked.

For example, when it comes to parenting, a person from a different race may assume that a White mom isn't committed to disciplining her child because she allows him to run around the church building. But this mom grew up in a legalistic home that was overly strict, and she is eager not to make the same mistake with her own kids.

Your brother from an African American background may never volunteer his home to be used for fellowships. One could assume that he's being selfish—but you'd be more understanding if you realized that he grew up in a very private African American family that rarely had people that they didn't know over to the house.

Meanwhile a White sister wants to share a meal to be gracious and thoughtful to a Latino family—but the receiving family may not be interested because they come from a tight-knit culture where only the extended family prepares meals in times of need.

In all these situations, it would be tempting to look at one another and simply say, "You're wrong." But instead we need to recognize that people have different experiences and upbringings, and come from various cultural backgrounds that shape how they interpret life.

This is why we all need the Scriptures to help us reinterpret our experiences. Bringing our own preferences to God's word allows us to check them as we do life together: "Is this value I hold dear commanded by Scripture, or is it merely my cultural preference?"

The question that we must ask is: Will my bias hinder love? Will my perception of my brother's or sister's parenting, or their readiness to invite others to their home, or their willingness to accept meals from others create a suspicion within me and cause me not to love them?

Let the Scriptures help us humbly accept one another and our respective experiences: "Accept one another, then, just as Christ accepted you, in order to bring praise to God" (Romans 15:7, NIV).

4. We Walk Away When Things Get Messy

There are so many churches to choose from. If we don't like some particular facet of a church, we can freely move on to another. However, if that is something we're considering, we must ask ourselves: Am I leaving for biblical reasons or something else? Many times, we don't understand that church is messy. As one writer says, "If church does what it is intended to do, things are bound to get messy."[10]

It's messy for several reasons. First, the church is made up of sinners who are seeking to do life together. We are redeemed, but we're still works in progress. No matter

---

10 Gregory Coles, "Church is Supposed to be Messy", https://www.crosswalk.com/church/pastors-or-leadership/church-is-supposed-to-be-messy.html (accessed September 18, 2024).

how long we've been saved, we are still being sanctified. Second, some people in the church are not yet believers. They are sinners with no Holy Spirit. This is bound to cause congregational chaos. Third, the gospel will reveal messiness in our hearts. It turns the light on broken places that need sanctification—we begin to see the messiness that we might once have overlooked. Fourth, an active enemy is provoking and stirring up commotion against the kingdom of God. We have a real enemy that likes messes.

If that is what happens in regular, culturally homogeneous local churches, can you imagine what can happen if you add different races, ethnicities, and cultures into a church? Doing life among multiple ethnicities can be messy as well. We come to the church with different preferences, expectations, familiarities, traditions, desires, biases, histories, upbringings, longings, and so on. But for it to work long-term, there has to be buy-in to stay devoted to one another and love each other through the messiness. For a multiethnic church to become a loving family, people must trust Jesus and the work of the Holy Spirit in the messiness of living among one another.

OVERCOMING THE BARRIERS

Amid the reality of these barriers to unity, it's essential to remember one crucial truth: Christ is in the barrier-breaking business. These obstacles will not thwart his church. Our question is: Where do churches find the power to be both multiethnic and loving families?

1. Own Our Past

In the US, our past as a nation can cloud our enthusiasm for becoming a multiethnic church. Contributing factors for African Americans are a 400-year history of slavery, emancipation, segregation, Jim Crow, Civil Rights, and desegregation. The late Toni Morrison was an American author, editor, and professor who won the 1993 Nobel Prize. Speaking of America she said, "In this country, American means White. Everybody else has to hyphenate."

Many African-American, Latino, and White believers haven't given up hope that multiethnic church is possible. But an honest assessment of where the church has been is critical for progress, along with a genuine willingness to consider the implications of that.

Frankly, the American church has not historically been committed to unity. We must be honest: racism is part of America's sordid past—both inside and outside the church.

Sin is real, but the God of heaven redeems his people from all iniquity. Repentance in Christ leads to right standing with and complete forgiveness from God the Father. Reconciliation is to be a significant posture and purpose of God's people. Remarkable unity can be achieved through the power of the gospel. However, as a body, we must own our past, mistakes, duplicity, and complicated responses and humbly rely on the Holy Spirit through the gospel to forge a path forward.

2. Embrace a Robust Understanding of the Gospel and Its Implications

The gospel is God's power to bring us safety, joy, and contentment in the presence of God for all eternity. It saves us from God's wrath, gives us Christ's righteousness, and secures for us an eternal home in heaven. Without Christ, we were dead in the trespasses and sins, following the course of this world (Ephesians 2:1-2). God, being rich in mercy because of his great love for us, has made us alive in Christ (v 4-5). Christians have been saved by grace through faith and adopted into the family of God to live with him forever. We didn't deserve it, earn it, or perform for it. It was a gift of mercy given by a merciful Savior. Now indwelt by the Holy Spirit, we live to the praise of his glory. We can't be a loving family without this understanding of the gospel.

3. Commit to Intentional Connection across Cultures

At the end of most church services, the people who know one another or hold things in common typically cluster together to talk after the service. Choosing a community group is often no different. People want to be with those that they like or have something in common with. In the early days of our multiethnic church, people would build friendships with people who looked like them.

Knowing the implications of this pattern long-term, as a leadership we consistently encouraged people to connect with someone who didn't look like them. To help this happen, we made our community groups geographically based. This forced people to spend time and do life with all kinds of people in different seasons. Also, people started eating one another's food—discovering the culinary beauty of various cultures was a win for everyone!

In our church, people are encouraged to sit with people they don't know at men's and women's events. When it comes to pastoral visits, we seldom pair an elder with a member of the same race unless it's impossible to avoid. Our ministry teams are diverse, creating an opportunity for interaction, teamwork, disagreements, and sharing love. G.K. Chesterton says, "We have never even begun to understand a people until we have found something that we do not understand. So long as we find the character easy to read, we are reading into it our own character."[11] To create space for love, we must put people in a position where they can learn new ways of doing things with those they wouldn't necessarily select to love. Intentionality creates such an opportunity.

4. Foster a Culture of Grace

The ethic of the gospel is grace. Having received grace, we give grace. We give grace not to the deserved but to the undeserved. As mentioned earlier, the multiethnic church can be messy. But the pursuit of multiethnic unity is worth the risk of messiness. When it gets messy, our

---

11 G.K. Chesterton, *What I Saw In America* (ebook edition, Floating Press Publisher, 2011), p 156.

response must be one of grace. But this doesn't happen by chance; it's a culture we must foster—a culture that allows people to make mistakes, say the wrong things, get offended, ask "stupid" questions, be oversensitive, and in all these things be met with grace.

We constantly need reminders to extend grace to one another based on the grace that has been extended to us in Christ. In a multiethnic church, the need remains. When African American people say the wrong thing, extend grace. When White people ask questions that may be misunderstood as racist, extend grace. When Latino and Asian people say something that may hurt someone's feelings, extend grace. If there's one place on earth where we don't get canceled and ostracized for making mistakes, it should be the church. Let's foster a culture of grace in our churches that is so impactful and relationally unifying that the world asks the church for help.

5. Commit to Practical One-Anothering

As mentioned in chapter 4, the Scriptures are full of commands for us to care for one another. But the one-anothers of Scripture mean nothing if we aren't committed to practicing them in the lives of brothers and sisters who are different from us.

For example, when a White woman chooses to build up and honor an African American leader, something powerful happens within the church. Why is this the case? It's life-giving for a multiethnic church because she is choosing to obey God's command to honor her leader. Or what happens when an African American woman spurs on her White sister by perpetually encouraging her? Or when the majority culture willingly serves ethnic minorities among them?

Practically speaking, I've seen this at work in my church. Unleashing the one-anothers radically fueled us towards becoming a unified and loving family. We must rely on the robustness of the gospel to see all believers as the family of God because, for years in America, we haven't. But when the one-anothers are at work, our apathy is shaken, and a vibrant and engaged loving family replaces the segregated church. We don't want to merely have a diverse church service. We want a loving family.

LIVING OUT THE LAMB'S DREAM

After this I looked, and behold, a great multitude that no one could number, from every nation, from all tribes and peoples and languages, standing before the throne and before the Lamb, clothed in white robes, with palm branches in their hands, and crying out with a loud voice, "Salvation belongs to our God who sits on the throne, and to the Lamb!" (Revelation 7:9-10)

One day, people from every nation, from all tribes and peoples and languages, will stand before the throne and the Lamb. But we don't have to wait for heaven, as glorious as that day will be! Instead, let's rejoice in the opportunity to humbly reflect the heavenly reality on earth now, even as we look forward to experiencing it in full one day.

If you ever have the privilege of attending a Panthers game, amid the diverse crowd cheering on their respective teams, remember this: God's bride, his church, can become a multiethnic, loving family—clothed not in Carolina blue but in the white robes of the Lamb—living out his dream for us.

ACTION STEPS

- Reflect on where your church is in its journey toward becoming a loving multiethnic family. What grounds do you have for encouragement? In what ways do you need to grow? Then ask someone from a different cultural background to yours how they see things.

- Consider whether there are ways in which your worship gatherings and community life as a church could better reflect the diversity of your members.

- Learn more about your nation's history as it pertains to race relationships. Ask others for recommendations of books, articles, documentaries, and podcasts that will introduce you to new points of view.

- Seek to build meaningful connections with church members who are from a different cultural background than you.

7. OUT OF THE CHURCH
AND INTO THE WORD

What kinds of questions would you ask when moving to a new neighborhood? Maybe: "How good are the local schools?" "What amenities is it near to?" "How far is it is it from my job?" "Will I be close to friends and family?" Or "What is the crime rate, and will I be safe?" In other words, we want to know whether a prospective neighborhood will bring us benefit or not.

On one level, that's reasonable. But Jesus would have us ask another question of the places in which we live and lay down roots: How can I bring blessing to this place? Jesus wants his people to be salt and light in the world (Matthew 5:13-16). We are called to be conduits of blessing rather than cul-de-sacs of benefit. We are called to love our neighbors, not looking for something from them but looking to extend something to them—namely, the good news of Jesus.

So far in this book, we've mainly thought about how we can love and care for one another within the family of

God. But now it's time to go one step further and ask ourselves: How can the people of God be a blessing to those around them? How can we extend the love that we have received towards others who don't know Jesus? How can we be the salt of the earth and the light of the world to the communities around us?

WHEN LOVE COMES IN, WE MUST GO OUT

The answer starts, as ever, with looking to Jesus, our Savior, and how he moved toward us. John 1:14 says:

> *The Word became flesh and dwelt among us, and we have seen his glory, glory as of the only Son from the Father, full of grace and truth.*

Jesus was incarnated among us—that's a fancy word meaning that he become human and dwelled with us. It's as we properly appreciate and understand this reality that we'll increasingly become blessing-bringers rather than benefit-seekers. Because God came to us, we go to others.

And why did God come to us? One pastor put it like this: "Jesus moved into our neighborhood, not because it was a great place to live—it was very much a 'step down' from his previous residence. But he did it for us… to be with *us*. He did it because he was on a rescue mission to save us and bring us into his family."[12]

---

12 Steve Sage, "Jesus Moved Into the Neighborhood"; https://graceredeemer.com/jesus-moved-into-the-neighborhood/ (accessed September 18, 2024).

The God of heaven left heaven behind. He became a man so that we could have direct access to him. He took up residence among the regulars. He made himself at home in the neighborhood. He revealed the visible presence of God to humanity by engaging with common, everyday people. He spent time with tax collectors, prostitutes, widows, orphans, and the impoverished. The point is that Jesus didn't only hang out with those who could benefit him; he hung out with those who needed him.

In the same way, I'm called to engage with those I can't get something from. Jesus' incarnation compels me to likewise move toward the world in love. His love frees me from my self-centered benefit-seeking and turns me outward to selflessly bless others.

VISION CHECK

Let's allow Jesus' incarnation to act as a litmus test for our lifestyle as believers and churches. What does your lifestyle say about your understanding and embracing of the gospel? If the incarnation doesn't fuel you to reach outward toward others, you're missing something. Gospel love for others is the natural outworking of a gospel-fueled life.

If God's love has truly moved into the church, the church must move into the neighborhood. As the Father sent Jesus into the world, so Jesus sends us, his people (John 20:21). Here are two sets of questions to help you examine your heart:

1. Are you moved with compassion for the lost around you? Does the eternal plight of the nonbeliever stir you? Do you ache with a desire for them to receive what you've received?

2. Where does that desire for others "take on flesh"? Who are you meeting? Who are you rubbing shoulders with? Are you declaring the good news of Jesus with your words and displaying God's character in your deeds?

In chapter 1, we thought about Jesus' words in John 13:35: "By this all people will know that you are my disciples, if you have love for one another." The question, though, is this: where are they going to see us loving one another if we don't go out to them? It's so easy to become "army-base Christians"—we drive our cars out of our garages to go to church, where we hang out with "our people"; and then we drive our vehicles back into our garages so that we can hang out with "our people" at home.

But there's a war going on outside. The enemy is waging war against souls. God has commissioned us to share the soul-freeing love we've received. It's urgent.

Instead of driving in and out of garages, only thinking about what benefits us, we must see ourselves as planted by God in our neighborhoods. We are here to bring the presence of God to those around us. God divinely positions us in neighborhoods on purpose. When we believe this, we'll see the world's darkness through Jesus' lens, and we'll step into it in hope, with the light of the gospel in our hands. We'll move toward our neighbors rather than away from them.

By the way, when I talk about "neighbors," I'm not thinking only of those who live immediately next to us. There are lots of ways to meet people in your local community. Wherever we are, if we are there, God has us there to get to know and reach people! For example, every Saturday, an amazing number of people gather to watch their kids play sports at an open field near my house. I used to play basketball at the YMCA, and that was a great way to get to know people too.

Additionally, many of us have jobs that create opportunities in the workplace. As we build relationships with coworkers, we're in a position to hear their concerns, problems, pains, and stressors—moments of honesty that move us toward them with compassion.

As we move toward people with the gospel, we can do so with confidence. Why? Because we've experienced Jesus coming to us in our brokenness. If he did that for us, he is powerful enough to do it for them too. As a verse in one of my favorite traditional African-American songs says, "If he did it before, he can do it again." So we look ahead to the transformation that God can bring and prayerfully step into the lives of others, asking God to make much of himself, to work, and to shine. If we are influenced by the incarnation of Jesus, by God's grace, he will use us to have a gospel impact in our neighborhood.

DISPLAYING JESUS' LOVE TO THE NEIGHBORHOOD

Here are four postures to help you display Jesus' love to your neighborhood.

Engage

First, we seek to participate in what's going on around us and in people's lives. We intentionally choose to go where they are and hang out. Where we might once have chosen to do an activity in a manner disconnected from people, instead we decide to connect with our neighbors. We do it voluntarily and vulnerably. No one forces us to. We don't do it begrudgingly.

As we engage with people, we seek to understand what's going on in their lives. We listen. We ask thoughtful and sincere questions. We talk about what interests them. We ask about what they've been up to. "How's the family? What have you been doing lately for fun?" We listen to see how we can be a kind and loving neighbor to them. We might seek to have parties, movie nights, birthday celebrations, and cookouts to get to know them and to celebrate together.

I remember being invited to a Christmas party in the neighborhood. My wife and I almost didn't go. As for most families, the holidays are hectic for us. But we wanted to engage with our neighbors. So we went to the party and had a blast. We all shared updates on our kids. We heard how our neighbors had experienced hardships, including job losses, illnesses, and death within their extended family. We laughed, joked around, and told funny stories. If we hadn't gone to that party, we would have missed engaging deeply with our neighbors. These connection points were invaluable to my wife and me, and over time they developed lasting relationships of trust and friendship.

How could you seize the opportunities to get to know people in your community?

Embrace

Your neighbors are people with feelings just like you and I. They experience hardships. They receive difficult medical diagnoses. They lose loved ones. They struggle with depression, anxiety, and discouragement.

As those who are planted in the neighborhood, we should be sympathizing with them. Crying, mourning, and weeping with our neighbors is our privilege. With genuine concern and unconditional love, we deliberately listen to their hearts' cries. We offer them our presence and comfort. We bring Christ's kindness to them.

It's as we serve our neighbors as individuals and as a church that they realize what the family of God looks like. Some people will never attend church, but in our care for them, we get to show them, with humility and compassion, what they miss out on. We offer them an "open house"-type view of church community. But for that to happen, we must embrace our neighbors with action.

A few years ago, my neighbor told me that his mom had cancer. I prayed for her as often as I remembered, but the cancer led to her death. I knew the pain, heartache, and grief he must be feeling, based on the loss of my own mom. So when I found out, I told him that if there was anything that he needed, I was available for him. I gave him a sympathy card with some money without waiting for him to ask it of me. I cut his grass while they were out of town. I raked his leaves. I gathered his mail. When he returned, I asked whether we could prepare meals for him and his family. I wanted him to know that his mom's life mattered, and so did his.

A familiar thing happened with Sarah, a janitor at the middle school that our church rented. She too lost her mom. As a church, we were heartbroken by how quickly it happened. We loved Sarah. She told us as she was preparing the funeral that she didn't have enough money to bury her mom. Immediately, as a church, we wrote her a check for $500, and a few of our members attended the funeral. Sarah was blessed and never stopped thanking us for supporting her during this difficult and painful season.

Serve

Our neighbors have practical needs that we can meet. I'm not just talking about the need for milk, sugar, and batteries, or to use your lawn mower, although it's beautiful to share these. They also have unspoken and even more profound needs that may require time, patience, and humble persistence to unearth. Don't assume that you know what they need. Prayerfully ask God to help you build such a relationship with your neighbors that they answer you honestly when you ask, "What do you need?" It's hard to know what someone needs from a distance. When we are up close and personal, we uncover needs.

I remember when it was very windy during a stormy day here in Charlotte, and I had to run outside to ensure my gutters were draining water through my runoff pipes. When I was checking mine, I noticed that my neighbor didn't have any way to prevent the water from seeping into his foundation. A few days later, I purchased a runoff hose for his gutter. This simple purchase and act of kindness was easy and low-cost, but my neighbor appreciated it when he noticed it shortly thereafter.

Or, thinking more broadly, what are the needs in your town or city that stir your heart? Recently my wife and I have been burdened by the homeless population in our area. At many stoplights, we see men and women holding signs that say, "Homeless, please help!" Or, "STARVING." What can we do? How can we serve them? Currently, we are making plans to purchase a stack of generic gift cards to have in the car to give them, which they can spend on food and other necessities. We've also talked about having snacks and water, or even meals, that we can hand them out of the window to remind them that they are seen and loved.

Another way to serve and move toward people in your community is by volunteering within organizations that reach out and serve the disadvantaged. For instance, I know several women from my church who offer their time and service to the local crisis-pregnancy center. Doing so gives them an opportunity to serve pregnant women but also gives space for building relationships and being a witness of love and hope.

How else could you find out what the community needs? Perhaps there is a town hall meeting or a residents' association meeting that you could attend. Maybe there are ways you could be a blessing to local schools. Here, in the United States, teachers often become especially weary between February and April—this three-month stretch doesn't have many breaks. So for several years, I've dropped off sandwiches, gift cards, and donuts in the teacher's break room on behalf of our church. They are always surprised and delighted to receive our gesture of kindness.

Are there ways you could act as a church to serve your community? For example, a few years ago, when the middle school that we were meeting in at the time experienced budget cuts, they asked us if we could contribute to them being able to wax the entire school's floor. We paid for all the wax so that the school could be ready for the opening of the school year. It was a way to say, "We care about this school, and we care about this community."

Stay

People in the neighborhood want to know whether we will be present for the long term or are just passing through. They likely don't want to waste time building relationships if we aren't committed long-term. As we develop friendships, we need to be dedicated to the people. Our goal isn't to change the neighborhood but instead to become an expression of Jesus' presence. So be all-in. Be a steady presence. Take up residence where God plants you.

And if it gets hard or crime goes up, don't take the easy road out by leaving unless God says so. Even when people who don't look like you move into the neighborhood, don't move away. Stay put and ask God to equip and empower you to be God's ambassadors. Play the long game.

This isn't merely about us as individuals but about us as church communities too. We serve the community in prayerful hope that all types of people from all different social backgrounds would come to know Jesus as Savior and Lord. We want to build a long-standing church that our great-grandchildren will attend. We want our kids and grandkids to be discipled and for them to seek to evangelize future generations in our city and beyond.

Of course, it's not always possible to stay. As a church, after eleven years of meeting in a middle school, we eventually had to relocate to a high school eight miles away because our lease was terminated. We would have loved to have stayed in that neighborhood, but we sensed this was God's plan. But for those eleven years, we loved our community. We engaged, embraced, and served. We stayed as long as God would have us there. We fought the temptation to move away for any reason other than God's best. We committed ourselves to be a present witness, and we believe that God honored that.

LET LOVE FLOW

These four postures are not a strategy to guarantee specific results if you adopt them for long enough. But God does do extraordinary things when we engage, embrace, serve, and stay in our communities. So we surrender to this incarnational lifestyle, although it looks countercultural, trusting that it will begin to bring about gospel impact.

What happens when the people of God are filled with the love of God and move out from the bounds of their church walls into their neighborhood? People who were once dead in their sins are made alive in Christ. Neighborhoods darkened by sin and brokenness that are often ignored by churches are invaded with the light of the gospel. Slowly but surely, God builds a people from all types of places—people who were once dead, now alive, worshiping King Jesus and giving their lives away in service to the King.

When gospel love flows from the church into the world, broken, curious, and doubting people meet Jesus through his incarnational army of redeemed followers. When people experience who Jesus is, their lives are never the same. This is the reason why love must move out!

ACTION STEPS

- Seek to engage with folks in your neighborhood. You could start by simply taking a walk without headphones and greeting the people you see.

- Consider how you could deepen your relationships with neighbors or other contacts such that you'd be in a position to see or ask about their needs. What would the next step in that relationship look like? (For example, stopping to chat, inviting them to your home, suggesting doing an activity together, asking for their help, etc.)

- Research what groups or organizations are seeking to meet needs in your community, and consider whether there is a way in which you could contribute.

- If there is a need in your neighborhood or city that God has particularly placed on your heart, start to pray intentionally about what it might look like for you and your church to respond. Ask God to provide brothers and sisters to join you in your endeavor.

8. OUR FUTURE HOPE

Three years after becoming a believer, I was invited by a trusted pastor to be a part of a leadership team in a church plant. At that stage, I didn't even know what a church plant was—but being part of the leadership sounded honorable and "grown-up."

I learned so much in that season about what godly leadership looks like. But I also learned how hard church life can be. I'll never forget when, five years in, a newly appointed treasurer became disgruntled with the lead pastor. He entered the room for a special meeting, clearly with something on his chest, and venom spewed out of him. Until this point, all I had experienced was love, respect, and kindness among the leadership team. But this was something different. Hatred flowed like a river. Accusations, allegations, blame, unkind words, anger, and disrespect filled the room. The lead pastor remained gracious, thoughtful, loving, and professional, but nothing helped this man. It was a hot mess. I quietly told myself, "If this is church leadership, I'm out." I was shaken.

We don't have to be in leadership to know that local church can be messy. We've spent seven chapters thinking about how the church should care for one another. But what do we do when our brothers and sisters fail to show that care for us? If you stick around any one church long enough, you'll doubtless have seasons of disappointment and disillusionment when you wonder, "How can I keep loving my church when it's this hard?" How do we cope with the hurt?

Thankfully, we are not the first to endure struggle and tensions as a church body. The apostle Paul, in his letter to the Romans, was writing to a church that was composed of both Jewish and Gentile followers of Jesus. They were trying to figure out how to live together as a family when they had such distinct differences of custom, preference, and practice. There was relational tension between believers on matters such as whether to observe holy days (Romans 14:5) and what food should or shouldn't be eaten (v 2). In addition to the internal tension, there were external pressures. Life in the Roman Empire brought suffering and persecution (5:3)—and suffering has a way of shifting our eyes off others and onto ourselves.

It would have been easy for the church in Rome to simply give up this dream of being a loving multiethnic body of Christ. They were likely asking themselves, "How can I keep loving my church when it's this hard?"

Tucked away in Romans 5 is a succinct answer to our question:

Therefore, since we have been justified by faith, we have peace with God through our Lord Jesus Christ. Through him we have also obtained access by faith into this grace in which we stand, and we rejoice in the hope of the glory of God. (Romans 5:1-2)

Immediately before these verses, Paul has been reminding the Romans of the story of Abraham—how he believed God's promise to make him the father of many nations, even amid impossible circumstances, and through him to bring blessing to the world. Romans 4 makes it clear that Abraham was made right with God through his faith in God's promise, not his works. Romans 5 continues by saying that our salvation comes the same way as Abraham's—through trusting in the promise of God rather than working for our salvation.

Verse 2 tells us a key blessing that flows from the reality of our salvation: "We rejoice in the hope of the glory of God." In other words, believers can look to what *will be* to empower them to get through *what is*.

While that exhortation was to Roman Christians struggling to endure in their faith amid persecution from those outside the church, the principle also helps us to endure in love with problems inside the church. In short, if Paul were talking to us, he'd say that the way to continue to love our church during the hard times of life on this side of eternity is to allow our future hope to fuel our present perseverance.

Let's break the text down for a second. Note that this is written to a body of believers—that they do this rejoicing together: "*We* rejoice in the hope..." This isn't something we're to do on our own; this is something that the body does as one—as a family. We rejoice together that there is a sure future hope.

So what does it mean to "rejoice"? The word can also be translated as "boast." The idea is of calling something to mind, cherishing it, and rolling it over and over again in our heads. It's like the savoring of a great meal—you eat it slowly, and you appreciate all the sights, smells, and tastes of it. "Rejoice" is not a "fast food" kind of word but rather a "crockpot" kind of word. Nor is it a one-off. We rejoice now and continue to do so.

Now, what do we, as a church continually, together rejoice in? The *hope* of sharing the glory of God. The author John Stott defined Christian hope as "a joyful and confident expectation which rests on the promise of God."[13] Because Jesus said, "It is finished" on the cross (John 19:30) and because he rose from the dead (Matthew 28:6), we as a church have a "good as done" hope. There is a zero-percent chance that the hope in which we boast will not come to pass. We, as the body

---

13 John Stott, *The Message of Romans*, The Bible Speaks Today series (InterVarsity Press, 2020), p. 127.

of Christ, have a sure hope in which to rejoice!

And what is that hope exactly? It is the hope of the *glory of God*. Another commentator, C.E.B. Cranfield, says that the glory of God is "that illumination of man's whole being by the radiance of the divine glory which is man's true destiny but which was lost through sin."[14] One day, when Jesus returns, our restored relationship with our triune God will be fully realized. We will share in the reality of all creation being restored to its original purpose, set free from sin (Romans 8:21), and all people who have been justified by faith through Jesus (Romans 5:1) will be restored to perfect enjoyment forever of the right relationship with God that he has secured for us. It will be glorious! This is the day that together we are to rejoice in and look forward to.

Imagine what kind of church you would be if you regularly rehearsed this reality together. As Stott says, "Our vision of future glory is a powerful stimulus to present duty."[15] Our future hope ought to fuel our present perseverance as a loving church in this world.

Yet, as much as we know this is what should be, years of church experience have taught me that this isn't always what happens. Things get in the way of us rejoicing in our future hope. Let's talk through some of these things.

---

14 C.E.B. Cranfield, *Romans: A Shorter Commentary*, International Critical Commentary on the Holy Scriptures of the Old and New Testaments (A&C Black, 2002), p. 103.

15 Stott, *The Message of Romans*, p. 128.

HINDRANCES AND HELPS

Hindrance 1: Delaying the Realization until Eternity

Unfortunately, there can sometimes be an unspoken feeling that we can wait until heaven to begin being a loving church. It's almost a sentiment of "We can't do this perfectly, so why even try?" In my experience, I've mainly seen this attitude arise in response to the challenge of loving across differences, such as race and class. The obstacles to unity seem insurmountable. We know that negotiating them will involve encountering wrongdoing, offence, disappointment and more. So we stop trying. "Being a loving church will never happen in this life," the thinking goes. "Why bother while we are on earth? Let's just wait for heaven when everything will be perfect."

Help 1: Think Invitation Rather Than Imperative

As followers of Jesus, God invites us to join him in his work as we pray and labor for God's kingdom to come on earth as it is in heaven. Granted, this is something he *commands* of us (so not doing it isn't an option). But it's also helpful to see this as an *invitation* to join God in his work and live closer to the fullness of joy together that we will one day have.

If you're attempting to persevere in loving your church during hard times purely because it's something you *have* to do, then you're unlikely to do it with joy, and you're likely to miss its present blessings. But when you view this call as something, by God's strength, that you *get* to do, your attitude will be transformed. You'll be much more likely to look to Jesus' strength to get you through, and when you do, you'll experience God's power to sustain you through the difficulties. You'll see the fruits that come from holding on—fruits like restored relationships between brothers and sisters that you'd never thought possible, people growing in their faith, saints sacrificially serving one another in a way that demonstrates Christ's love, and more. You'll have the eyes to see what Jesus is doing at the moment, rather than gritting your teeth and just "getting through it."

If your heart says, "Well, I can't do it perfectly, so I'll wait until heaven," you must ask yourself why. Why don't you want to live out, even in part, what one day will be perfected? If love and unity is where we're heading, what does it say about your heart that you're not willing to strive for it right now?

The beautiful thing, though, is that the sacrifice and loving commitment of your church today helps you rejoice in what's coming. It's like a movie preview that we get to experience here on earth. As we persevere in loving one another, we are invited to have a foretaste of our glorious, certain future as a perfectly united body in Christ.

Hindrance 2: A Culture of Boasting in the Temporary

Oftentimes, the things that are talked about and celebrated most in our churches are things other than the sure hope of the glory of God. While we would intellectually affirm that boasting in our eternal hope is most important, what we actually boast about in real-time is often far more earthly. We might rejoice in our church's growth or our style of church (that music that we just love!). Or we rejoice in our advances in our jobs, the achievements of our kids, our trips at the weekend, and our prosperity here on earth. These are all good things—but what we must realize is that, though we're not saying it out loud, these temporal boasts can cause people to think that when things on earth go south, something is wrong.

What we talk about most passionately is reflective of where our most profound hopes are. If we're rejoicing to one another more about the here and now rather than our confident hope of the glory of God, our fortitude to endure through relational disappointment will be depleted.

Help 2: Boast in What Lasts

Jesus told his disciples that the kingdom of heaven is worth giving up everything else that you have in order to gain it: "The kingdom of heaven is like treasure hidden in a field, which a man found and covered up. Then in his joy he goes and sells all that he has and buys that field" (Matthew 13:44).

We need to practice rejoicing rightly with one another. We are to rejoice in the coming glory with Jesus more than we boast in temporal things. That way, when things don't go the way we want here on earth, we aren't shaken. If someone criticizes us, we're not crushed beyond hope—because their approval wasn't our treasure. If someone lets us down, we don't pull away—because that person wasn't holding the weight of our hopes. When we are going through something and it seems that no one else knows, we don't grow bitter—because our ultimate hope is in God's eternal care for us.

As we rejoice in our hope in Jesus, we can commit to being together through thick and thin and ups and downs. We can choose presence together over preferences being met. We know there's treasure of great value in the kingdom of heaven, and we're committed to uncovering it together.

Hindrance 3: The Option to Depart When Things Get Hard

One challenge for the present-day church in the West is that we have so many options of where we can attend. We can leave a church and go to another one down the street. This choice frees us from any real demand to stay when relationships are challenging. Unlike the Christians Paul addressed in Rome, who likely only had one Christian community they could be a part of, we've got options. Rather than confronting the sin in front of us, or owning and repenting of ours, we can escape any awkwardness by going elsewhere.

Now, I'm not saying that there are never reasons to leave a church. Sometimes things can be so harmful that it is time to leave, especially if the leadership is complicit or active in the dysfunction. That is not what I'm talking about here. What I am saying is that far too often, folks leave a church due to the challenges posed by people rather than a conviction from God that he's moving them on. For most of us, God is inviting us to persevere. So, we're back to the question: Why would you stay with a church when things get hard?

Help 3: Open Yourself up to Formation

Romans 5 goes on to assure us that present suffering—of whatever kind—isn't pointless. Rather, it is purposeful.

> Not only that, but we rejoice in our sufferings, knowing that suffering produces endurance, and endurance produces character, and character produces hope, and hope does not put us to shame, because God's love has been poured into our hearts through the Holy Spirit who has been given to us. (Romans 5:3-5)

Our future hope empowers us to rejoice in present suffering, knowing that this produces all kinds of character formation, with the result being a deeper conviction of our hope—which will not disappoint us.

Leaving a church too early short-circuits this process of spiritual formation. If we leave, we may forfeit the experience of knowing God in hardship. We may bypass the potential for deeper connections with other believers. We may forgo the opportunity for growth and trust in Christ. Unknowingly even, we may exchange serving others for serving self. We may miss out on the joy of witnessing to others such that they come to faith.

If you want to grow stronger in your faith and your confidence in what is to come, stick around with a faithful church and commit to love them. Over time, by the work of the Spirit, you will realize that God is doing some major formation in your heart.

ALL THINGS NEWS
So, where does this leave us?

I hope that, as you finish this book and seek to love your church in the present, your eyes will be fixed on the future. That, after all, is where God leaves us at the close of the New Testament: with a vision of the eternal future reality that will be brought about when Jesus comes back.

> And I heard a loud voice from the throne saying, "Behold, the dwelling place of God is with man. He will dwell with them, and they will be his people, and God himself will be with them as their God. He will wipe away every tear from their eyes, and death shall be no more, neither shall there be mourning, nor crying, nor pain anymore, for the former things have passed away." And he who was seated on the throne said, "Behold, I am making all things new." (Revelation 21:3-5)

I can't wait to hear that loud voice thunder from the throne. The God of all things—who was, and is, and is to come—will one day, finally and fully, dwell with his people as he intended from the start. And this won't be a temporary tabernacle; this will be an eternal abode, with no expiration date, where he and I and all who call upon the name of Jesus for their salvation will dwell.

On that day, we will no longer be hoping or striving to love our church. We will perfectly love the people of God, for we will perfectly love God. We will be forever that which Jesus lived and died to make us—a people for God's own possession (1 Peter 2:9), who will eternally declare his praise in perfection. And all the challenges of being part of a loving-but-still-sinful church on earth—the tears, the hurt, the confusion, the frustration, the suffering—will be done away with. And we will look back on it all and say, "Worth it." What a day of rejoicing this will be!

But let's not wait until then to rejoice as his body. Here and now, because Christ lived perfectly, died in our place, and rose victoriously, we can "rejoice in hope of the glory of God" (Romans 5:2). And that "hope does not put us to shame, because God's love has been poured into our hearts through the Holy Spirit who has been given to us" (v 5). He keeps us, and he keeps our church family, from the day of our conversion to the hour of Christ's return. Let's rejoice in this hope, together.

ACTION STEPS

- In your conversations with other Christians this week, notice what you are "boasting" about or rejoicing in. Seek to increasingly point yourself and others to the "hope of the glory of God."

- Reflect on your attitude towards church community. Is there any part of you that has given up on pursuing relationships of love and care? Why might this be?

- If you've been part of your church for a while, write a list of all the ways that you have seen the Spirit bearing fruit in the people around you, such as reconciled relationships, growth in faith, sacrificial service, and more. Spend time thanking God for how he's been at work, and let others know that you're thanking God for them too.

- Make a second list of ways in which you'd like God to form your character in the year ahead, as you persevere with your church family. Pray through it, and then put it in an envelope somewhere safe. Set a reminder on your phone to look at the list again in a year's time, and see how God has answered your prayer!

DISCUSSION GUIDE
FOR SMALL GROUPS

1. WHY LOVING THE CHURCH MATTERS

1. Share about a Christian whose example of care for others has shown you the Lord Jesus.

Read John 13:1-17, 34-35

2. What is the benchmark for how Christians ought to love one another (v 34)? Why is that a high bar?

3. In verse 15, Jesus says that his actions are an example for us. What does Jesus' washing of the disciples' feet reveal about what Christian love looks like?

4. What does Jesus promise will be the effect of loving other disciples (our church family) like he does (v 34-35)?

5. To what extent is your church known for how you love one another? Can you think of a time when your care for each other impacted the watching world?

2. WHAT GETS IN THE WAY OF CARING FOR ONE ANOTHER?

1. How would you have answered the question above before you read this chapter? How about now?

Chapter 2 considered how our lack of love for others stems from our love for something else: idols.

Read Exodus 32:1-6; 1 Corinthians 10:1-14

In this section of 1 Corinthians (8:1 – 11:1), Paul is answering a question about whether it was okay to eat food sacrificed to idols.

2. What is idolatry, and what makes it so dangerous?

3. "Idolatry would never be a problem for me." How would you answer a statement like that from a Christian, based on this passage?

4. Pages 33-34 mention four idols: significance, comfort and security, power, and money. How might each of those lead you to fall short in caring for your brothers and sisters in Christ? What other idols might be a problem for you?

5. Consider the sections toward the end of the chapter on racism, politics and social media. Which of these were you most personally challenged by, and why?

6. What encouragement do you find in these verses in our fight against idolatry? (For additional encouragement, read 6:9-11.)

3. LOVED BY A LOVING SAVIOR

1. Can you think of a particular time when an awareness of God's love for you helped you to love someone else?

Read Hosea 11:1-11

2. Based on this passage...

   • how had God shown his love for his people, Israel, in their past?

   • how does he express his love for them in Hosea's day?

   • how does he promise that he will show his love for them in the future?

3. What about us today? (If you can, recall New Testament Scriptures that speak into each of the following.)

   • How has God shown his love for his people, the church, in the past?

   • How does he express his love for us in the present?

   • How does he promise that he will show his love for us in the future?

4. "If this is how God has loved us—and if this is his posture toward the brothers and sisters we gather with Sunday by Sunday—how can we not seek to love others in the same way?"(p 48). In what specific ways is your love for God's people different than his is? In what ways would you like to change and grow?

4. ONE-ANOTHERING IN ACTION

1. Share about a time when you've seen your church rally around a member in need.

Read Colossians 3:12-17

2. Identify all the different things believers are called to do for one another in these verses.

3. What does it mean that love "binds everything together in perfect harmony" (v 14), do you think?

4. Pages 57-59 talk about serving one another in the church with our money, words, time, and gifts. Which of those is the area where you most need to grow, and why?

5. Take the opportunity to honor and encourage one another right now! Tell another member of your group how you've noticed them serving and loving others, or using their gifts, in a way that you've found personally encouraging.

6. What's one thing that you want to do this coming week that will put what we've learned about one-anothering into action? Check in next time you meet to see how it went!

5. UNCONDITIONAL LOVE IN A DIVIDED CULTURE

1. What would you say are the big issues in your culture that currently cause the most division?

Read Ephesians 2:11-22

2. What previously divided the Ephesians before they became believers?

3. How has that now changed, according to Paul? Talk through all the different steps that made the Ephesians' new unity possible. How would they have needed to have lived differently as a result, do you think?

4. How can we tell the difference between "love" that's actually based on reciprocity or uniformity and love based on the unity of the gospel?

5. As you look at your church and your own heart, in what areas and on what issues do you think you are at most danger of division?

6. Which of the "Five Dynamics of Unconditional Love" on pages 73-79 did you find most helpful, and why?

6. WHEN MULTIETHNIC CHURCH BECOMES A LOVING FAMILY

1. Where would you need to go to witness the most diverse gathering of people in your city or community?

Read Acts 2:1-14, 29-47

2. In what way was the church at the end of Acts 2 more diverse than at the beginning of the chapter? What was it that brought them together?

3. What marked them out as a loving family (v 42-47)?

4. What issues might this increasingly diverse church family have had to work through as time went on? (You could draw on your knowledge of Acts.)

5. How do you think your church is doing regarding the dual aims of 1) being a multiethnic family; 2) being a loving family? What signs of encouragement can you thank God for? In what areas do you need to ask for his help to grow?

6. Which of the barriers to becoming a loving family, described on pages 85-91, do you think your church is currently grappling with?

7. What is one practical thing that you want to do as an individual to forge meaningful connections with brothers and sisters who are different than you? What could you do together as a group?

7. OUT OF THE CHURCH AND INTO THE WORLD

1. What do you love about the community you live in?

Read John 1:1-18

2. According to these verses, in what ways was Jesus' incarnation—his coming to live among us—so extraordinarily radical?

3. What would it look like for us to live in our community with a similar attitude, posture, and mission to the one displayed by Jesus, as described in this passage?

4. "It's so easy to become 'army-base Christians'" (p 102). Is this a temptation for you? In what ways?

Consider the four postures for displaying Jesus' love in your neighborhood described in this chapter: engage, embrace, serve, stay.

5. Where do you think you're currently at in that process as an individual? What would the next step (or the first step) look like for you? Is there a group or individual whom God has laid on your heart?

6. Where do you think you're currently at in that process as a church? What would the next step (or the first step) look like for you collectively? How could you help to make it happen?

7. OUR FUTURE HOPE

1. When are you most tempted to give up on caring for God's people?

Read Romans 5:1-11

2. What does Paul say that believers are to do, in light of the truth of the gospel (v 2, 3, 11)?

3. What temporary things are you personally most tempted to "boast" in? What about as a church?

4. What would it look like to increasingly boast in Christ instead?

5. If you're able to, share about a time in your life when walking through a hard season with your local church formed your character in good and God-honoring ways.

6. Read Revelation 21:2-4. How do these verses grow your hope in God's plans for his people?

7. Looking back over the whole book, what truth about God do you most want to hold on to? What action step do you most want to continue walking in?

RESOURCES FOR
SMALL GROUPS

Access the free small-group kit at loveyourchurchseries.com. The free kit includes PDF versions of the book's discussion guide. Additional small group kits for other books in the series are also accessible, some of which include videos and worksheets.

loveyourchurchseries.com

ACKNOWLEDGMENTS

To my sweet wife, Leslie: your unwavering love, commitment, support, and encouragement have blessed me. I truly cherish you and your sacrifices throughout this ministry journey. Thank you for being my greatest cheerleader.

To my brother and writing coach, Doug Logan: the countless hours you have invested in me and your wisdom and encouragement have impacted my life. You have sharpened me and helped me be a better man.

To Jake Mitchell: thank you for your exceptional editing, attention to detail, and commitment to excellence. I greatly appreciate your partnership and support with this book.

To Tony Merida: I am grateful for your trust in me, your encouragement, and your invitation to join this writing journey. Your friendship and support are blessings I genuinely cherish.

And to Wellspring Church: thank you for allowing me to lead and serve you. Walking with you, guiding you, and building a community of care and support with you has been one of the greatest joys of my life.

Thank you all.

LOVE YOUR CHURCH

loveyourchurchseries.com

BIBLICAL | RELEVANT | ACCESSIBLE

At The Good Book Company, we are dedicated to helping Christians and local churches grow. We believe that God's growth process always starts with hearing clearly what he has said to us through his timeless word—the Bible.

Ever since we opened our doors in 1991, we have been striving to produce Bible-based resources that bring glory to God. We have grown to become an international provider of user-friendly resources to the Christian community, with believers of all backgrounds and denominations using our books, Bible studies, devotionals, evangelistic resources, and DVD-based courses.

We want to equip ordinary Christians to live for Christ day by day, and churches to grow in their knowledge of God, their love for one another, and the effectiveness of their outreach.

Call us for a discussion of your needs or visit one of our local websites for more information on the resources and services we provide.

Your friends at The Good Book Company

thegoodbook.com | thegoodbook.co.uk
thegoodbook.com.au | thegoodbook.co.nz
thegoodbook.co.in